21st CENTURY

LIFESKILLS

MATHEMATICS

Smart Shopping Math

SADDLEBACK
EDUCATIONAL PUBLISHING
www.sdlback.com

ISBN-13: 978-1-61651-406-8
ISBN-10: 1-61651-406-X
eBook: 978-1-61247-000-9

Printed in the U.S.A.

20 19 18 17 16   6 7 8 9 10

Table of Contents

Unit 5: Getting the Best Deal

Unit 6: On-line Shopping

Unit 7: Shopping for a Neighbor

Unit 8: Second Time Around

Teacher's Notes and Answer Key 105

To the Student

Welcome to *Smart Shopping!* This is Book 5 of the *21st Century Lifeskills Mathematics* series.

The goal of this book and the other books in this series is to build your confidence and practical math skills. You will use these math skills in everyday situations throughout your life.

You solve problems and make mathematical decisions every day. You compare products and make choices about what to buy. You work to earn money. You decide what to spend and how much to save.

21st Century Lifeskills Mathematics gives you strategies to solve everyday math problems in a variety of ways. It strengthens your skills and gives you practice with many different math topics. Each of the six books presents topics you are likely to encounter in everyday life. Each book includes problems that involve estimation, equations, mental math, calculators, and critical thinking. Each book includes additional topic-specific skills such as graphing, averages, statistics, ratios, and measurement.

Each unit begins with a preview lesson, which models and explains the types of problems you will encounter in the unit. Then there are five lessons, at least one of which is usually a game. Each unit ends with a review of the unit concepts. There are illustrations and graphic art throughout.

Here is a list of the titles of the other books in the *21st Century Lifeskills Mathematics* series:
Book 1: Everyday Life
Book 2: Home & School
Book 3: On the Job
Book 4: Budgeting & Banking
Book 6: Sports, Hobbies, & Recreation

With review and practice, you will build your math skills and learn to approach everyday mathematical situations with confidence! *21st Century Lifeskills Mathematics* will help you become a successful problem solver!

Unit 1

Retail & Wholesale

Preview

How You Will Use This Unit

As you think about retail and wholesale shopping, you will consider many different things. Price and selection are two examples. You will probably also consider retail outlets and closeout sales. You may also think about co-ops. As you compare options and make choices, you will often use math. The math skills you use include mental math and estimation, basic operations and equations, statistics and probability, ratios and proportions, and graphs.

What You Will Do in This Unit

In this unit, math steps demonstrate how to solve problems. These steps can help you answer questions such as these:

SneakerDeals is holding a sale. The first pair of sneakers costs $54. The second pair costs half that amount. The next pair costs half that amount again, and so on. How does the mean cost per pair change, as the number of pairs increases?

Out of a stack of 60 dinner plates, you find five that you like. Suppose that you find the same fraction of mugs in the stacks of mugs. How many mugs do you find?

A flyer reads, "Purchase items for as little as 15% of the retail cost." You buy a swimsuit for $11. The retail tag reads $72. Does this item meet the flyer's promise?

You compare the prices of items at the food co-op and the supermarket. You want to know the answers to two questions. For which item is there the greatest difference in price between the two stores? At which store is $20 enough money to buy one of each item on your list?

What You Can Learn from This Unit

When you complete this unit, you will have used mathematics to work problems related to retail and wholesale shopping. These problems are similar to those that may actually occur in your daily life.

Lesson 1

Retail Deals

Example *ShoeDeals* is holding a shoe sale on its discontinued lines. The first pair of shoes costs $36. The second pair costs half that amount. The third pair costs half the amount of the second pair, and so on. Draw a graph to show the relationship of the number of pairs of shoes a person buys to the total cost of their purchase. How does the mean cost per pair of shoes change as the number of pairs increases?

Solve

Step 1: Make a table to show the total cost of 1 to 5 pairs of shoes.

Number of Pairs of Shoes	Sum of Individual Costs	Total Cost	Mean Cost per Pair
1	$36	$36	$\frac{\$36}{1} = \$36$
2	$36 + $18	$54	$\frac{\$54}{2} = \$27$
3	$36 + $18 + $9	$63	$\frac{\$63}{3} = \$21$
4	$36 + $18 + $9 + $4.50	$67.50	$\frac{\$67.50}{4} = \$16.88$
5	$36 + $18 + $9 + $4.50 + $2.25	$69.75	$\frac{\$69.75}{5} = \$13.95$

Step 2: Now draw a graph. First label the horizontal axis as "Number of Pairs," and the vertical axis as "Total Cost." Next, plot the data from the table. Graph the number of pairs of shoes (*x*-axis) against the total cost (*y*-axis).

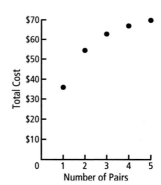

Answer the Question

Step 3: The mean cost per pair of shoes decreases as the number of pairs increases.

✏️ Now try these problems.

1. Joris sees a sale on camera lenses. The first lens costs $168.75. The second lens costs two thirds of that amount. The third lens costs two thirds of the second, and so on. Joris buys three lenses.

a. Complete the table to show the total cost of his purchase.

Number of Lenses	Sum of Individual Costs	Total Cost
1	$168.75	$168.75
2		
3		

b. What is the difference between the cost per lens for three lenses and the cost of the first lens? $_____

2. Tami organizes the bookstore's annual sale of overstocked items. Books are on sale for $2 each. CDs and DVDs are on sale for $3 each. How much money does the bookstore make when they sell all the CDs and DVDs? How many books do they need to sell to equal that amount? Draw and label a bar on the graph to represent this number.

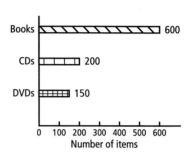

Answer: The bookstore makes $_____ when they sell all the CDs and DVDs.

They need to sell _____ books to make the same amount of money.

3. On Saturday, all display pottery items are on sale at 75% off. JoAnn and Linda each buy several items and spend a total of $95. How much would they have spent before the sale?

   A $71.25   **B** $126.67   **C** $380.00   **D** $475.00

4. Over the holidays, the town of Fan holds an annual *ShopAround*. The town's only trolley car makes an hour-long circle around town. Shoppers can get on and off at six different stops. Daren gets on the trolley at 10 a.m. At each stop, he gets off, spends half an hour, and then waits until he can get on again. Circle the time at which he gets back to his starting point.

   11 a.m.   12 p.m.   1 p.m.   2 p.m.   3 p.m.   4 p.m.

☆ Challenge Problem
You may want to talk this one over with a partner.

Where you live, you can buy sweet corn at any time of the year. But the cost varies, from $0.05 per ear to $1.00 per ear. Draw a double line graph to show the cost per ear for one to ten ears at each of these two prices. How do the two graphs differ?

_____

_____

Lesson 2

Visiting the Outlets

Example Bridget visits the wholesale district to look for bargains. In *Elegant Tables,* she hunts through the stacks of china for her patterns she likes. Out of a stack of 60 dinner plates, she finds five that she likes. She looks through stacks of 50 salad plates, 88 bowls, and 72 mugs. Suppose she chooses these items in about the same proportion as the dinner plates. How many pieces of each item does she find?

Solve

Step 1: Write the ratio of the number of dinner plates she chooses to the total number of dinner plates in the stack.

$$\frac{5}{60} = \frac{1}{12}$$

Step 2: Underline the sentence that tells you the assumption for finding the number of other items.

<u>Suppose she chooses these items in about the same proportion as the dinner plates.</u>

Step 3: Use the ratio of dinner plates to write a proportion that gives the number of pieces of each of the other items.

$$\frac{\text{(Chosen salad plates)}}{\text{(Total number of salad plates)}} = \frac{1}{12}$$

Chosen salad plates $= \frac{1}{12} \times 50$

$\qquad\qquad\qquad = 4 + \text{remainder of } 2$

Chosen bowls $= \frac{1}{12} \times 88$

$\qquad\qquad\quad = 7 + \text{remainder of } 4$

Chosen mugs $= \frac{1}{12} \times 72$

$\qquad\qquad\quad = 6$

Answer the Question

Step 4: Bridget finds 4 salad plates, 7 bowls, and 6 mugs.

✎ Now try these problems.

1. In *SportsOutlet,* Coe hunts through a pile of tracksuits. From a selection of 16, he finds four that he likes. Suppose he finds pairs of sneakers in the same proportion as the tracksuits. Write a proportion and solve it to find the number of good pairs of sneakers, *s*, out of a selection of eight.

   Answer: _____ / _____ = _____ / _____   s = _____

2. In *Music's*Out,* Marcile hunts through the rack of CDs. From one rack of 40 CDs, she finds seven to buy. Suppose she finds the same number of DVDs from a selection of 28. Write a word sentence and an expression for the fraction of DVDs that she will buy.

   Answer: _____

3. Ricardo often buys fruit and vegetables at the farm stand near work. The price is two thirds of what he would pay at the regular supermarket. Today he spends $4.50 for 7 pounds of apples and two pumpkins. What would he have spent at the regular super-market? Label his produce with this dollar amount.

Congratulations! You would have paid $_____ at the regular supermarket!

4. Terri reads the table on the wall over the 'seconds' stand. How many items would she purchase to get the lowest mean price per item?

Number of Items	1	2	3	4
Price	$15	$25	$35	$45

   A 1   **C** 3

   B 2   **D** 4

☆ *Challenge Problem*
You may want to talk this one over with a partner.

It takes you one hour and a gallon of gas to get to the outlet mall. You stay three hours and pay $1.25 per hour for parking. The trip home costs you another hour and another gallon of gas. You pay $1.68 per gallon for gas. Suppose you have a seen a sweater that you like for $40 in a local retail store. How much does a similar sweater have to cost in an outlet store to make the trip worthwhile?

Answer: A similar sweater has to cost less than $_____.

Lesson 3

Liquidation & Closeouts

Example When Ross goes downtown, he makes his trip pay for itself by visiting discount shops. He records his expenses and estimates his savings based on typical retail store prices. The table shows the results of one of his trips. This trip takes him four hours. He spends $2.50 on gas and $0.75 on parking. How much does the trip earn him in savings per hour?

Source	Item	Cost	Estimated Savings
Everything Wholesale	50 pounds of cat food 4 gallons of generic shampoo/conditioner 25 pounds of generic detergent	$16.75 $15.80 $6.25	$0.99 $12.90 $9.40
Tex's Liquidations	12 12-ounce cans of orange juice 24 12-ounce cans of cranberry juice	$6.50 $15.60	$3.00 $8.50
Yard Sales	Winter jacket Box of old CDs	$2.00 $3.00	$62.00 $60.00

Solve

Step 1: Calculate the total amount Ross estimates that he saves on the items he purchases.

$0.99 + $12.90 + $9.40 + $3.00 + $8.50 + $62.00 + $60.00 = $156.79

Step 2: Now subtract the cost of gas and parking to find the actual amount he saves.

$156.79 − $2.50 − $0.75 = $153.54

Step 3: Now calculate his savings per hour.

$\frac{\$153.54}{4} = \$38.39$ Divide by the number of hours that the trip takes.

Answer the Question

Step 4: The trip earns Ross $38.39 in savings per hour.

✏️ Now try these problems.

Refer to the information in the example as you work the first problem.

1. When Ross goes downtown, he makes his trip pay for itself. The table in the example shows the results of one of his trips. On his *next* trip, he buys the same items at the same prices at *Everything Wholesale* and *Tex's Liquidations*. He does *not* catch the yard sales. But he does visit a discount sports store where he buys a pair of sneakers

for $28.97, instead of $98.99. This trip takes him five hours. He spends $3.00 on gas and nothing on parking. Complete the sentences to tell how much this trip earns him in savings per hour?

Answer: Total Savings = $_____ – $_____ = $_____

This trip earns Ross $_____ in savings per hour.

2. Charlcie picks up a flyer as she walks into the sports store closeout sale. The flyer reads, "Purchase items for as little as 15% of the retail cost." Charlcie picks up diving accessories for $35. The tags say the total retail price for these items is $175.

   a. Add symbols to complete the math sentence that gives Charlcie's percent saving.

   Answer: Charlcie's percent saving = $35 ___ $175 ___ 100 = _____%

   b. Do the items meet the flyer's promise of 15% discount? If not, by how much is the promise off?

   Answer: _____

3. Every two months Fayrene closes *DeepDiscounts* for one month to go in search of new liquidated stock for the store. What portion of the year is the store closed?

   A $\frac{1}{4}$ **C** $\frac{1}{2}$ **B** $\frac{1}{3}$ **D** $\frac{2}{3}$

4. In *Dings&Dents,* Berto finds a suitcase for one fifth of its regular retail price, reduced because of a scratch. He pays $45 for the suitcase. He also finds a sports bag for $37, reduced from its regular retail price of $111. Circle the correct entry in each column.

Regular price of suitcase	Percent the sports bag is reduced	Total that Berto saves
$135	20%	$82
$180	33.3%	$254
$225	66.7%	$336

☆ *Challenge Problem*
You may want to talk this one over with a partner.

You and a friend go downtown on a shopping trip. You visit eight different stores, and pay $3.25 for parking and $4.50 for gas.

a. What is the mean cost of the trip per person, excluding the cost of the items that you buy?

Answer: Mean cost of the trip per person is $_____.

b. What is the mean cost of the trip per store?

Answer: Mean cost of the trip per store is $_____.

♖ A Board Game (for Two Players)

The goal of this game is to cover (or buy) sets of cells on the board. First, you look for four cells that are not covered. Then you place a purchase coupon over these four cells.

Materials

Game board (on the next page), 24 purchase coupons (on the next page)

Directions

1. Put the purchase coupons so each player can reach them. Sit with players on opposite sides of the game board.

2. Player 1 picks a purchase coupon and places it over four cells on the game board.

3. Player 2 then takes a turn, picks another purchase coupon and places it over another four cells. A player cannot place a purchase coupon over four cells if one or more cells are already covered.

4. Players take turns picking and placing purchase coupons.

5. The winner is the last player to place a purchase coupon on the board.

✏ Before you play the game, try these warm-up problems.

1. After three turns, how many cells on the game board will be covered?

   Answer: _____

2. Yancy has made six plays, and Zarek has made five plays. Yancy could only make another move if he covers a cell that is already covered. How many cells are still uncovered on the game board? Explain why neither player could be able to make another move.

   A 20   **B** 30   **C** 34   **D** 44

   If neither player can make another move, it could be because

   _____

   _____

   _____

Game Board for *Strategic Purchases*

Purchase Coupons

Make 8 of each: 2-by-2 squares, 4 dog-legs, and 4 rectangles.

Lesson 5

Co-ops & Clubs

Example Haydn makes a bar chart to compare the prices of four items at the food co-op and the local supermarket. The quantity of each pair of items is the same.

a. For which item is there the greatest difference in price? For this item, what percent of the price of the higher-priced item is the price of the lower-priced item?

b. At which store is $20 enough money to buy one of each type of item and receive change? How much change? (No tax is charged on food items.)

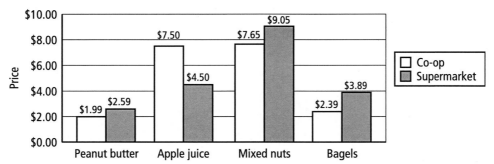

Solve

Step 1: Where is the difference in the heights of the two bars the greatest? Which item do these two bars compare? Read the two values off the chart and compare them. Then calculate the percent.

$$\frac{\$4.50}{\$7.50} \times 100\% = 60\%$$

Step 2: Add the prices of the items from the co-op and then those from the supermarket. Calculate the change from $20.

Co-op: $1.99 +$7.50 + $7.65 + $2.39 = $19.53. Change = $0.47.

Supermarket: $2.59 + $4.50 + $9.05 + $3.89 = $20.03 He will owe 3 cents.

Answer the Question

Step 3: a. The supermarket price for apple juice is 60% of the price at the co-op.

b. At the co-op, Haydn can buy one of each type of item and receive $0.47 change from $20.

✏️ Now try these problems.

Refer to the information in the example as you work these problems.

1. Haydn looks at the prices of the items again.

   a. Which item is about the same price at the co-op and the supermarket? For this item, what percent of the price of the higher-priced item is the price of the lower-priced item?

   Answer: The item for which there is the least difference in

   price is _____.

   The price of this item at the _____ is

   _____ of the price of the item at the _____.

   b. He only wants to shop at one of the two stores for apple juice and mixed nuts. He has a $10 bill, a $5 bill, and 2 nickels. At which store can he afford to buy these items? How much change will he receive? (No tax is charged on food items.)

   Answer: He can afford to buy apple juice and mixed nuts at the

   _____. He will receive $_____ in change.

2. According to authorities, one in every three citizens in the United States is a member of a co-operative club. Draw and label a circle graph to represent this information.

3. Kendra is a member of an art co-operative. For art supplies, she saves 20% of the price that a non-member would pay. On average, Kendra pays about $45 per month for art supplies. What would she have paid over the course of one year if she were not a member?

   A $56.25   **B** $225   **C** $540   **D** $675

4. Lexi pays $35 a year for a warehouse club membership. Jason is not a member of the club, but he can shop there and pay a 5% surcharge on purchases. How much does Jason have to spend before a membership could save him money?

   Answer: $_____

☆ Challenge Problem
You may want to talk this one over with a partner.

You pose the following puzzle to a friend. Three prime numbers, d, e, and f satisfy the following two conditions: (1) $d + e = f$ (2) $1 < d < e$.
What should your friend's answer be when you ask for the value of d?

Answer: _____

Review What You Learned

In this unit you have used mathematics to solve many problems. You have used mental math and estimation, practiced basic operations, and solved equations. You have also used statistics and probability, ratios and proportions, and graphs.

These two pages give you a chance to review the mathematics you used and check your skills.

✔ Check Your Skills

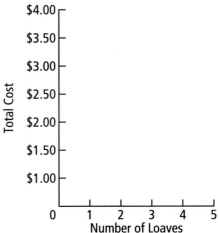

1. *Breads4Life* sells day-old bread at deep discounts. The first loaf costs $1.50. The second loaf costs half that amount. The next loaf costs half that amount again, and so on. Fill in the graph to show the relationship of the number of loaves of bread a person buys to the total cost of their purchase. How does the mean cost per loaf change as the number of loaves increases?

   Answer: _____

   _____

   If you need to review, return to lesson 1 (page 2).

2. In *Tools Tools,* Aledro hunts for a tool kit. Out of eight different tool kits, he finds three that would satisfy his needs. Suppose he finds the same number of battery-powered hand drills from a selection of six. Write a sentence in words, and an equivalent math sentence, for the fraction of battery-powered hand drills that satisfy his needs.

   Answer: _____

   If you need to review, return to lesson 2 (page 4).

3. Macy picks up a flyer as she walks into the sports store closeout sale. The flyer reads, "Purchase items for as little as 20% of the retail cost." Macy buys a swimsuit for $18. What would the retail price have to be, to meet the flyer's promise?

   A $9   **B** $36   **C** $45   **D** $90

If you need to review, return to lesson 3 (page 6).

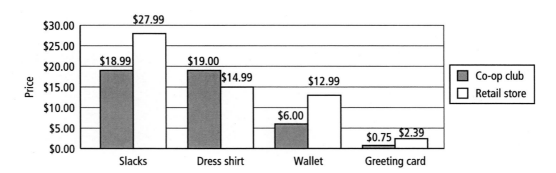

4. Bond compares the prices of four items at the co-operative club and the large retail store.

   a. Which item is about the same price at the co-op and the retail store? For this item, what percent of the price of the higher-priced item is the price of the lower-priced item?

   Answer: For _____, the percent that the cheaper item

   is of the more expensive item is _____.

   b. At which store is $60 enough money to buy one of each item and receive change? How much change? (No tax is charged.)

   Answer: At _____, Bond can buy each

   item and receive $_____ change.

   If you need to review, return to lesson 5 (page 10).

Write Your Own Problem ✍

Choose a problem you liked from this unit. Write a similar problem using a situation and related facts from your own life. With a partner, share and solve these problems together. Discuss the mathematics and compare the steps you used. If you need to, rewrite or correct the problems. Write your edited problem and the answer here.

_____

_____

_____

_____

Preview

How You Will Use This Unit

As you think about reading ads, you will consider many different things. You may ask: What is the ad really offering? What will the opportunity cost? You will probably also consider whether the information is misleading. You may search the ad for the fine print and read it carefully. As you compare options and make choices, you will often use math. The math skills you use include mental math and estimation, basic operations and equations, statistics and probability, ratios and proportions, and graphs.

What You Will Do in This Unit

In this unit, math steps demonstrate how to solve problems. These steps can help you answer questions such as these:

The headline for an article in the local paper reads: "Average donation so far $25. Can you match it?" Why might this headline be misleading?

An ad in the paper reads, "$17,500 is the top fee earned on one client this year ($2,000 average)." You wonder how many clients were placed, and what the other fees were.

You see the ad for $AZ Company, and track its stock market performance. You buy 100 shares of stock on 5/13, and sell all 100 shares on 5/17. Do you make or lose money?

You rush to the store for the half-price sale. The store ad reads, "Second item at half price!" The first pair you pick out costs $15; the second item costs $28. What is the bill?

What You Can Learn from This Unit

When you complete this unit, you will have used mathematics to work problems related to interpreting ads. These problems are similar to those that may actually occur in your daily life.

Lesson 1 ⟶ *Misleading Data*

Example The headline for an article in the local newspaper reads: *"Average donation so far $25. Can you match it?"* The actual data upon which the writer based this headline is shown here. Why might this headline be misleading?

Donations
$100
$25
$10
$5
$5
$5

Solve

Step 1: The term "average" can be one of the three measures of central tendency. Use the data from the chart to calculate each measure.

Mean: $100 + $25 + $10 + $5 + $5 + $5 = $150
$150 ÷ 6 = $25

Mode: $5   the number that occurs most often

Median: $7.50   the middle value when the data are listed in order.
This median is halfway between $10 and $5.

Step 2: Find each measure of central tendency for the data. Consider the differences and what the reader might think.

Mean: The writer used the mean value of the data.

Mode: The reader could interpret that most people made a donation of $25.

Median: The reader could interpret that the donation in the middle was $25.

Step 3: Explain why this might be misleading.

The reader might think "average donation" refers to the mode or median. Then the reader would have too high an idea of the average amount.

Answer the Question

Step 4: The headline could mislead because the writer chose to say "average" instead of "mean." The reader might think that most people made a donation of $25. This interpretation is wrong.

✐ Now try these problems.

1. At a local fund-raising group meeting, Galen tells the group that the average donation is $55. The group has collected the following donations: $100, $100, $100, $10, $10, $10. Does the data match Galen's statement? Explain possible misinterpretations.

Answer: _____

2. As part of the city's safety campaign, the PR committee creates a poster saying, *"Most accidents happen within 25 miles of home! Drive carefully!"* Which could best explain why this statement could be misleading?

   A The majority of journeys start and end within 25 miles of home.

   B People drive more carelessly within 25 miles of home.

   C The mean average is 25 miles. But the most frequent distance is less.

   D Most accidents happen within 5 miles of home.

3. Peri opens some mail from a music company. The headline to one ad reads, *"Over 1,000 titles for only $1, $2, or $3!"* The cost of shipping and handling is mentioned, in small print, on the other side of the ad. Peri calls and orders 3 $2-CDs and 3 $3-CDs. Why might she be surprised when she gets a bill for $21.95?

   Answer: _____

4. The high school posts a chart showing the average number of student absences for each month. The chart starts at the beginning of each school year. Which is the best explanation of why this chart could be misleading?

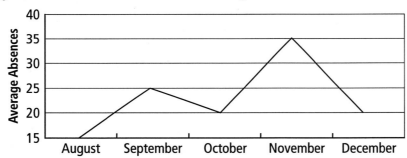

   A The school should use a bar chart.

   B The vertical scale starts at 15.

   C Attendance varies by month.

   D The total student population is ignored.

☆ *Challenge Problem*
You may want to talk this one over with a partner.

Refer to the information in problem 4 as you work this problem. One school emphasizes attendance. Why might the school want to use the graph in problem 4?

_____

Lesson 2

Reading the Classifieds

Example This ad catches Wesley's eye: *"$17,500 top fee earned on one client this year ($2,000 average over all our clients)."* Wesley wonders how many clients the company had this year. He also wonders what the mean (average) fee earned per client was (leaving out the one top client fee listed in the ad). What are the worst case answers to his questions?

Solve

Step 1: Suppose the firm had n clients. Represent the average dollars earned on all those clients but the top one as C. Then you can write this sentence.

(overall average) × (all clients) = (top fee) + (average of other clients) × $(n-1)$

so $\$2,000n = \$17,500 + C(n - 1)$

or $\$2,000n - \$17,500 = C(n - 1)$

The money made minus the top fee must be positive. What number for n makes the left side positive?

Try 8. No, 8 would mean that their fees (other than the top one) would be a negative.

Try $n = 9$. Then $\$18,000 - \$17,500 = C(9 - 1)$ and $8C = \$500$.

So $C = \$62.50$

Step 2: Next, make a conclusion about the minimum number of clients and the mean (average) fee for all clients except the top one.

The minimum number of clients is 9. The mean of all the other fees is $62.50.

Answer the Question

Step 3: The least number of clients placed this year was 9. The mean (average) fee earned per remaining client was $62.50.

✏ Now try these problems.

1. An ad in the newspaper reads, *"$8,500 is the top fee earned on one client this year ($1,200 overall average). Consultants needed! We do the work; you get half the fee!"*

   a. Bailey wonders how many clients were placed this year.

   Answer: The least number of clients placed this year = _____.

b. She also wonders what the mean (average) fee earned for the *other* clients was.

Answer: The mean fee earned per client (excluding the top fee) =

$\underline{\hspace{3cm}}$.

c. What would Bailey have earned as a consultant if she had been the consultant for *all* the clients this year? What are the worst case answers to her questions? (Round to the nearest dollar.)

Answer: She would have earned $\underline{\hspace{3cm}}$.

2. Josh scans the classified ads to find a used car. One ad reads, *"5 years old. Only 30,000 miles. $4,500 as is."* A second ad reads, *"2 years old. 20,000 miles. $6,000."* What is the difference in annual mileage between the two cars?

    A 3,000 miles   **C** 6,000 miles

    B 4,000 miles   **D** 10,000 miles

3. Jamar wants to buy his girlfriend a puppy. He sees a classified ad that reads, *"Puppies for sale. $25 each, or best offer. Call after 5 p.m."* He decides to offer $20 for one puppy. If the sellers accept his "best offer," what fraction of the advertised price does he get the puppy for?

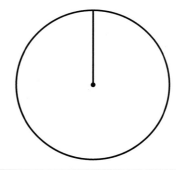

Answer: $\underline{\hspace{4cm}}$

4. In the real estate section of the classified ads, Helki reads, *"Home for sale by owner. Only $45,000."* She knows she might also have to pay a 6% realtor's fee in addition to the advertised price. What total price would she pay then? Circle the correct answer.

$6,000 $27,000 $42,453 $47,700 $72,000

☆ Challenge Problem
You may want to talk this one over with a partner.

You read the car ads in the classified section of the newspaper. Of the cars advertised, 8 cost $11,000 or more; 14 cost from $6,500 to $10,999; 25 cost from $3,000 to $6,499; 3 cost less than $3,000. Draw a circle graph to show this data. Write the percent of cars in each category.

Lesson 3

→ *Everyday Ads*

Example Benita sees the ad promoting $AZ Company. She tracks its stock market performance. She buys 100 shares of stock on 5/10, and sells all 100 shares on 5/20. Does she make or lose money? How much?

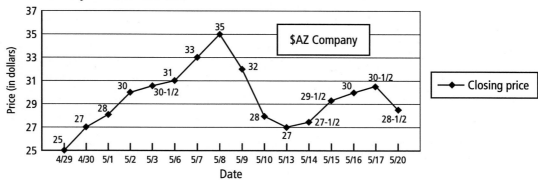

Solve

Step 1: Read the price of her stock off the chart on each of the dates.

5/10:   28
5/20: $28\frac{1}{2}$

Step 2: Underline the sentence that talks about her two transactions.

<u>She buys 100 shares of this company's stock on 5/10, and sells all 100 shares on 5/20.</u>

Step 3: Write an expression for the difference in dollars between when she buys and when she sells her shares.

$$(\$28.50 \times 100) - (\$28 \times 100) = \$0.50 \times 100$$
$$= \$50$$

Answer the Question

Step 4: Benita makes $50.

✏️ Now try these problems.

Refer to the information in the example as you work the first problem.

1. Shaina sees the same ad and tracks $AZ Company's stock market performance. She buys 50 shares of this company's stock on 5/13, and sells all 50 shares on 5/17.

    a. Write an expression for the amount of money that she makes or loses.

    Answer: (_____) – (_____)

---

b. Complete the sentence for the amount of money she makes or loses.

Answer: Shaina _____ (makes/loses) $_____.

2. Tait, Sven, and Lucas are ready for pizza. They look over the menu. List what they must do so that they pay no delivery fee and get a free soft drink.

	small	medium	large		small	medium	large
Pizza Plus	6.50	9.00	11.50	*Pasta*	5.45	6.50	7.25
Pizza Grande	7.85	10.50	13.75	*Sandwiches*	3.25	5.95	6.50
Today's Pizza	5.95	8.75	10.85	*Salads*	3.95	5.00	6.50

Free delivery with minimum order of $15.00.

Free
One 32-oz soft drink with purchase of a large pizza. Offer good only with delivery orders. *Offer expires 7/1.*

Answer: _____

_____

3. As a member of *ComputerWiz,* Fala sees an ad to order mousepads that display a color picture or photo. Fala wants to use the mousepads during an upcoming fund-raising event. What is the best price per mousepad that Fala can get?

Quantity	1+	Lots of 10	Lots of 25
Member cost	$5.50 each	$51.50 per lot	$118.75 per lot
Non-member cost	$6.60 each	$61.50 per lot	$133.75 per lot

A $4.75   **B** $5.15   **C** 5.35   **D** 5.50

4. Dawn looks at her picnic supply coupons. She has $11.50 in change. Circle the items that she can afford *and* save the most money.

Hot Dog Buns: $3.78 instead of $4.30.

Coleslaw for $2.50 instead of $2.70.

Franks for $5.89 instead of $7.00.

Potato salad for $2.88 instead of $3.13.

☆ *Challenge Problem*
You may want to talk this one over with a partner.

You study three toothpaste ads for toothpaste that normally costs $2.29 per tube.

a. Two tubes for the price of one, with the purchase of $10 or more of other products.

b. One free tube with the purchase of $20 or more of other products.

c. Buy one tube; get the second tube at half price.

What is the least amount of money you have to spend to get the best deal on the toothpaste? Explain your answer.

_____

_____

Lesson 4

Reading the Fine Print

Example Darcy rushes to the pet store for the half-price sale. The store ad reads *"Second item at half price!"* The first item that she picks, a pet bowl, costs $15. Her second item, a pet carrier, costs $58. Darcy is ready to pay $44, before tax. The cashier points to the fine print at the bottom of the ad. The fine print reads, *"Higher priced item at full price; other item at half price."* Before tax, what does Darcy pay for her purchases?

Solve

Step 1: Underline the sentence that gives the price of each item.

The first item that she picks, a pet bowl, costs $15. Her second item, a pet carrier, costs $58.

Step 2: Now underline the fine print.

"Higher priced item at full price; other item at half price."

Step 3: Write and solve an equation for the total cost of the items, before tax.

$58 + \frac{\$15}{2} = \$65.50$

Answer the Question

Step 4: Darcy pays $65.50, instead of $44, for her purchases.

✏️ Now try these problems.

1. Clem goes to the sports shoe store for the half-price sale. The store ad reads *"Second pair of sneakers at half price!"* The first pair that he picks out costs $24.99, and the second pair costs $98.99. Clem has $100 and is expecting to get change back after paying for his sneakers. The clerk points to the fine print at the bottom of the ad. The fine print reads, *"Higher priced pair at full price; other pair at half price."*

   a. What is the total cost of Clem's sneakers?

   Answer: Before tax, the total cost of the sneakers is $_____.

   b. What was Clem's mistake?

   Answer: _____

2. The headlines of a travel ad read, *"Book 4 nights or more and receive free companion airfare ... 4 days / 3 nights from $529."* Yves notes that the trip includes air fare; hotel; ground transportation; and hotel taxes. In fine print, he reads, *"All rates are per person, double occupancy."* Which statement is a reasonable assumption of what he can expect the total cost to be, if he invites a companion and pays for both people?

    A $529 more than $1,058

    B $529 plus one airfare

    C equal to or

    D $1,058

3. *ElectroniCity's* ad reads, *"10% off anything in the store AND a $15 welcome bonus!"* Taylor wants to buy a digital camera that regularly costs $249.99. He thinks he will only pay $209.99. The small print says, *"10% discount applies when you open a new ElectroniCity credit card account."* and *"$15 back by mail after your first credit card transaction."* Taylor does not want an *ElectroniCity* credit card account.

    a. Write an expression to explain Taylor's calculations to get $209.99.

    Answer: _____

    b. What price will Taylor really pay for the digital camera?

    Answer: $_____

4. Erin is making a reservation for a hotel room in Washington, D.C. One hotel advertises a room rate of $178 per night. In small print, Erin reads, *"All rates are subject to the Washington, D.C. tax of 14.5% per room per night."* Circle the amount that Erin will actually pay per night.

      $178 $108.58 $203.81 $258.10

☆ Challenge Problem
You may want to talk this one over with a partner.

How many pairs of two different negative integers can be multiplied to produce a product of 100? List the pairs.

Answer: _____ pairs: _____

Lesson 5

↱ A Graphing Game (for Two or More Players)

The goal of this game is to spend the least amount of money. First, you pick two cards. Then you calculate and plot the accumulated result on the graph.

Materials

Graphing game board (on next page), deck of discount cards, deck of price cards, counters in two or more colors, one for each player

Directions

1. Each player chooses a counter color. Shuffle and place both decks of cards on one side of the board. Sit with players around the game board.

2. Player 1 picks the top card from each deck. Apply the discount on the card to the price on the card. Then place a counter on the graph where the resulting price and the number of the round intersect.

3. Player 2 then picks a card from each deck and repeats the process.

4. Players take turns picking cards, making calculations, and placing counters on the game board for round number 1. More than one counter can be at the same place.

5. In the next round, each player adds the new calculated price to the previous price, and places a new counter for this total amount of money above the new number for the round. (This means that players accumulate the total amount of money they spend during the game.)

6. The game is over when one player reaches or exceeds $200 on the graph. Players connect their counters in a line graph. Compare and describe each graph.

✏ Before you play the game, try these warm-up problems.

1. On his first turn, Kito draws a discount card for 20% off and a price card for $50. Where on the board does he place a counter?

   Answer: _____

2. On his second turn Kito draws a discount card for 50% off and a price card for $40. Where does he place his second counter for round 2?

   A $20   **B** $30   **C** $60   **D** $80

Game Board for *Stretching Dollars*

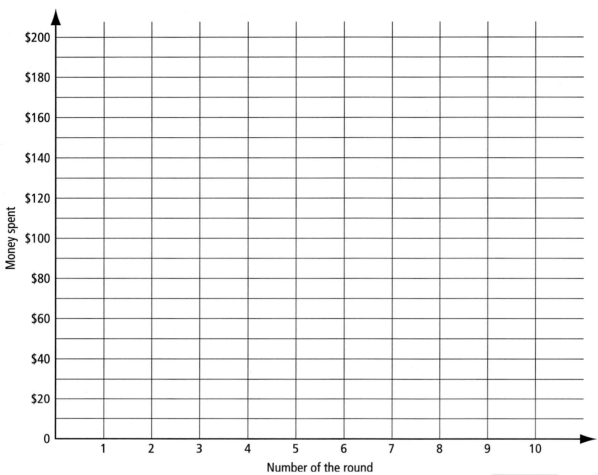

Money spent

Number of the round

Make up 3 discount cards each for the following savings: 5% off, 10% off, 15% off, 20% off, 25% off, 50% off, $2 off, $5 off, $10 off. **Be creative! Add more!**

Make up 3 Price cards each for the following original prices: $15, $20, $25, $40, $50, $60, $80, $100, $120. **Be creative! Add more!**

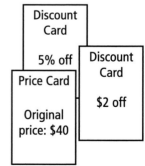

Discount Card

5% off

Price Card

Original price: $40

Discount Card

$2 off

Sample game

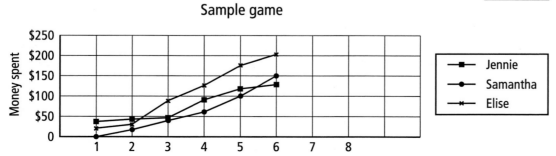

Money spent

- ■ Jennie
- ● Samantha
- ✕ Elise

Review

Review What You Learned

In this unit you have used mathematics to solve many problems. You have used mental math and estimation, practiced basic operations, and solved equations. You have also used statistics and probability, ratios and proportions, and graphs.

These two pages give you a chance to review the mathematics you used and check your skills.

✔ Check Your Skills

Donations
$400
$50
$40
$5
$5

1. The headline for an article in the local newspaper reads: *"Average donation so far: $100. Can you match it?"* The actual data upon which the writer based this headline is shown here. Why might this headline be misleading? Explain.

   Answer: _____

   If you need to review, return to lesson 1 (page 15).

2. An ad in the local newspaper reads, *"$21,000 is the top fee earned on one client this year ($1,500 average over all our clients). Consultants needed!"* Austin wonders how many clients were placed this year. She also wonders what the mean (average) fee earned per client was (excluding the top fee listed in the ad). What are the worst case answers to her questions? Fill in the blanks in each step to answer Austin's questions.

   Use ____ for the number of clients placed.

   Use ____ for the mean (average) fee per remaining client.

   Least number of clients placed = _____

   Mean (average) fee per remaining client = $_____

   If you need to review, return to lesson 2 (page 17).

3. Sumner graphs *CD$* Company's stock-market performance. He buys 25 shares of this company's stock on 5/3 and sells all 25 shares on 5/16.

   a. Referring to the graph on the next page, write an expression for the amount of money that he makes or loses.

   Answer: (_____) − (_____)

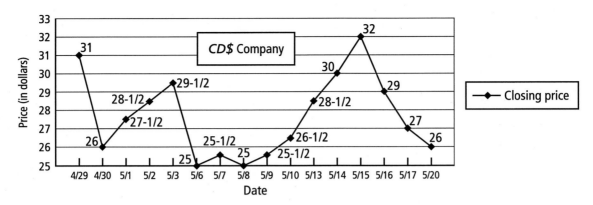

b. Complete the sentence for the amount of money he makes or loses.

   Answer: Sumner _____ (makes/loses) $_____.
   If you need to review, return to lesson 3 (page 19).

4. Lexia rushes to the kitchenware store for the half-price sale. The store ad reads *"Second item at half price!"* The first item that Lexia picks out costs $9.99, and the second item costs $21.45. Lexia is ready to pay $20.72, before tax. The cashier points to the fine print at the foot of the ad. The fine print reads, *"Higher priced item at full price; other item at half price."* What does Lexia pay for her purchases?

   A $15.72   **B** $20.72   **C** $26.45   **D** $31.44

   If you need to review, return to lesson 4 (page 21).

Write Your Own Problem ✍

Choose a problem you liked from this unit. Write a similar problem using a situation and related facts from your own life. With a partner, share and solve these problems together. Discuss the mathematics and compare the steps you used. If you need to, rewrite or correct the problems. Write your edited problem and the answer here.

Preview

How You Will Use This Unit

As you think about rental sales, you will consider many different things. Renting an apartment and renting movies are two examples. You will probably also consider renting items when you go on vacation. As you compare options and make choices, you will often use math. The math skills you use include mental math and estimation, basic operations and equations, statistics and probability, ratios and proportions, and graphs.

RENT NOW AND SAVE!

What You Will Do in This Unit

In this unit, math steps demonstrate how to solve problems. These steps can help you answer questions such as these:

You plan to go away for a week. You compare car rental ads in a travel magazine. What are the rental terms, and what is the maximum that you can save on car rental costs?

You belong to a movie club. The monthly charge is $15. You can download a movie whenever you want. In one month, you download ten movies. What is the cost per movie?

You hire Cerise to pet sit while you are away. Cerise charges $15 per day, or $85 per week. What condition makes the weekly rate more cost-effective than the daily rate?

While you are traveling, you rent out your home. You keep a record of your income (from your house and your job) and compare your total income from season to season.

What You Can Learn from This Unit

When you complete this unit, you will have used mathematics to work problems related to rental sales. These problems are similar to those that may actually occur in your daily life.

Example Vaughn goes away for a long weekend. He leaves on Friday, and returns on Sunday. He wants to rent an economy car while away, so he reads the ads in the magazine of his travel club. What is the maximum that he can save on car rental costs?

A | **Up to $20 OFF a Weekend or Weekly Rental!**
Weekend rentals must be for at least two days. Offer only good on mid-size or larger vehicle. You'll save $5 per day, up to $20.

C | **$20 OFF a Car Rental in Addition to Your Club Discount!**
Rent for a minimum of five days. You'll save $20 plus your club discount.

B | **Get Your Discount *and* Take $20 OFF any Weekly Rental!**
Rent for a minimum of five consecutive days. Offer not valid on economy cars. You'll save $20 plus your club discount.

D | **$15 OFF!
Any Car!
Any Day!**
Valid for a rental of at least two days. Offer valid on any size vehicle. You'll save $15!

Solve

Step 1: For each offer, list the conditions (minimum number of days and type of vehicle).

A: Minimum of two days. Good on mid-size or larger vehicle.

B: Minimum of five consecutive days. Not valid on economy cars.

C: Minimum of five days. Valid on any car.

D: Minimum of two days. Valid on any size vehicle.

Step 2: Circle the offer or offers that Vaughn can take advantage of.

Step 3: Underline the sentence that tells Vaughn how much he can save.

You'll save $15!

**$15 OFF!
Any Car!
Any Day!**
Valid for a rental of at least two days. Offer valid on any size vehicle. You'll save $15!

Answer the Question

Step 4: Vaughn can save a maximum of $15.

✏ Now try these problems.

Refer to the information in the example as you work the first problem.

1. After attending a weekend conference, Questa takes Monday through Wednesday for a vacation. She scans the ads in a magazine in the hotel lobby to find a reasonable car rental.

a. What is the maximum that she can save on car rental costs?

Answer: Questa can save $_____ on car rental costs.

b. Write the headline or headlines of the ads that give her the best cost.

Answer: _____

2. *The Bike Store* promotes their bikes-n'-binoculars package for more than just bikes or binoculars. In one week, they rent out their bikes 126 times. Two thirds of these bikes are part of the bikes-n'-binoculars package. Use the graph to complete the chart to show the missing data.

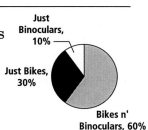

Package	Percent of rentals	Total bikes	Total binoculars	Total rentals
Bikes n' Binoculars	60%			
Just Bikes	30%			
Just Binoculars	10%			
Total	100%	126		

3. *TeenTown* rents its six seven-foot sailboats to earn money for teen activities. The rental is $20 per sailboat per hour, plus a deposit of $50. (Customers get their deposits back when they return sailboats undamaged.) On one Saturday, *TeenTown* rents four sailboats for eight hours each, and two sailboats for 5 hours each. All the sailboats come back with enough damage so that the deposit is not returned. How much money does *TeenTown* take in for their sailboat rentals that day?

    A $42   **B** $420   **C** $840   **D** $1,140

4. The Elisons hire *Dee's Catering Service* to cater a picnic for their family reunion. Dee charges $32 per hour for her time, plus the cost of supplies. She spends 3 hours shopping and $3\frac{1}{2}$ hours preparing food. Supplies cost $85.46. What is the total bill?

Answer: $_____

☆ *Challenge Problem*
You may want to talk this one over with a partner.

Weekend rates for a condo on the beach range from $1,500 during the high season to $600 during low season. Three blocks from the beach, rates range from $850 (high season) to $150 (low season). Are the high-season rates in proportion to low-season rates? Explain your answer.

Lesson 2

Renting Movies

Example *Couch Potato Heaven* rents DVD movies over the Internet for a monthly charge of $20. Their ad reads, *"Download and Watch Today!... No shipping, no late fee!"* Cappi decides this is a good deal. Over the first weekend, he downloads fifteen movies. Suppose that the average runtime per movie is about one and three quarters hours.

a. About how many hours will it take to run through all these movies?

b. What is the cost per movie for his movie entertainment so far this month?

Solve

Step 1: Underline the sentence that tells how many DVDs Cappi downloads.

Over the first weekend, he downloads fifteen movies.

Step 2: Next, multiply the number of DVDs by the average runtime per movie.

$15 \times 1\frac{3}{4}$ hours $= 26\frac{1}{4}$ hours

Step 3: Now divide the monthly charge by this number of movies.

$\$20 \div 15 = \$1.33$

Answer the Question

Step 4: **a.** It will take about $26\frac{1}{4}$ hours to watch all these movies.

b. The cost per movie for Cappi's movie entertainment so far is $1.33.

✏️ Now try these problems.

1. *MovieMania* rents movies over the Internet for a monthly charge of $25. Over the first weekend, Ash downloads ten movies. Suppose that the average runtime per movie is about two hours.

   a. About how many hours will it take to run through all these movies?

   Answer: It will take _____ hours to run through all these movies.

b. What is the cost per movie for her movie entertainment so far this month?

Answer: The cost per movie for her movie entertainment so

far is $_____.

2. Skelly rents a video from the "new release" stacks at the local video rental shop. He pays $4.99 and must return the video within 24 hours. Usually he rents an old release for $0.99 per weekend. Circle the approximate number of old releases that he can rent for the price of renting one new release.

3. Mandza borrows movies from the town library. The only charge is a late fee of $0.25 per movie per day. On Friday she takes out two movies. One movie is due back within 24 hours. The other is due back within 48 hours. On Monday, on her way to work, she drops the movies off. Write an equation that shows what Mandza owes for borrowing these movies.

Answer: _____ = _____

4. The students hold *"Movie Night"* in the park pavilion. They rent movie equipment for $75, plus a $25 deposit. (They get the deposit back when they return the equipment.) They buy sodas and popcorn for $50. The community lends old movies at no charge. The council sells n bags of popcorn for $1.25 per bag, and s cans of soda for $0.75. Which equation shows how much popcorn and soda they must sell to break even?

    A $0.75n + 1.25s = 150$ **C** $1.25n + 0.75s = 150$

    B $0.75n + 1.25s = 125$ **D** $1.25n + 0.75s = 125$

☆ *Challenge Problem*
You may want to talk this one over with a partner.

Circle any number that gives a lesser number when you take the square root.

$$-\frac{1}{4} \qquad 0 \qquad \frac{1}{9} \qquad \frac{4}{9} \qquad \frac{9}{16} \qquad \frac{25}{16} \qquad 25$$

Lesson 3

Rented Out!

✳ A Game (for Four or More Players)

The goal of this game is to fill up the game discs. You draw a rental card. Then you find a matching location on your game disc.

Materials

Game discs (at least one per player) and rental cards (see instructions for making cards on the next page)

Directions

1. Shuffle the rental cards and place the deck face down on the table. Sit with players around the table. Players pick a game disc to have in front of them.

2. Player 1 picks the top rental card. Look for a match on your own game disk. If there is a match, place the card close to that sector on your disc. If there is no match, place the card in your personal discard pile.

3. Players take turns picking the top card and placing them near their game disc or in their own individual discard piles.

4. The first round of the game is over when one player completes a game disc. That player can pick another disc to fill. Play as many rounds as you like.

5. The game is over when there are no more rental cards. Discuss its meaning: If each game disc represents a rental business, what do cards left in the discard piles mean? What do uncovered sectors mean? How could this help the owner of a rental business?

✐ Before you play the game, try these warm-up problems.

1. Jana owns the furniture/plant/art rental business (game disc). She has all sectors covered on her game disc except for the $299 furniture rental sector. If all but 15 cards have been played, what is the probability that the next card will be the right one? **Answer:** _____

2. Price picks a $15 Electric Car Rent card. (This means he has $15 that he would like to spend on renting an electric car.) What is the most likely reason that the rental business (game disc) does not offer this option? Discuss your answer.

   A A $15 rental is not profitable.

   B Gas costs more than $15.

   C This is not a business opportunity.

   D A competitor offers $15 rentals.

Game Discs for *Rented Out!*

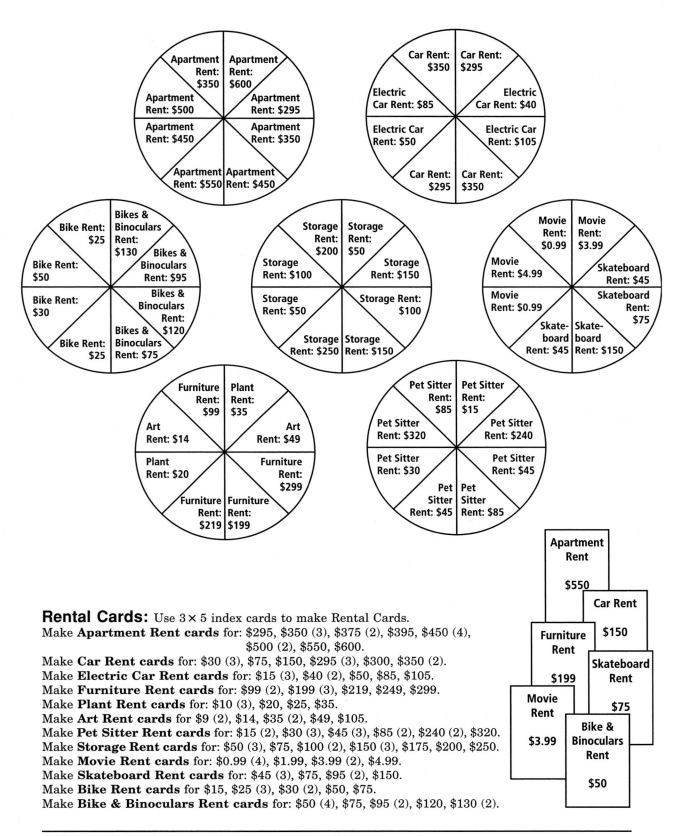

Rental Cards: Use 3 × 5 index cards to make Rental Cards.

Make **Apartment Rent cards** for: $295, $350 (3), $375 (2), $395, $450 (4), $500 (2), $550, $600.

Make **Car Rent cards** for: $30 (3), $75, $150, $295 (3), $300, $350 (2).

Make **Electric Car Rent cards** for: $15 (3), $40 (2), $50, $85, $105.

Make **Furniture Rent cards** for: $99 (2), $199 (3), $219, $249, $299.

Make **Plant Rent cards** for: $10 (3), $20, $25, $35.

Make **Art Rent cards** for $9 (2), $14, $35 (2), $49, $105.

Make **Pet Sitter Rent cards** for: $15 (2), $30 (3), $45 (3), $85 (2), $240 (2), $320.

Make **Storage Rent cards** for: $50 (3), $75, $100 (2), $150 (3), $175, $200, $250.

Make **Movie Rent cards** for: $0.99 (4), $1.99, $3.99 (2), $4.99.

Make **Skateboard Rent cards** for: $45 (3), $75, $95 (2), $150.

Make **Bike Rent cards** for $15, $25 (3), $30 (2), $50, $75.

Make **Bike & Binoculars Rent cards** for: $50 (4), $75, $95 (2), $120, $130 (2).

Example Martina hires Cerise to pet sit. Cerise charges $15 per day, or $85 per week. When does it cost less to pay the weekly rate than to pay the daily rate?

Solve

Step 1: Underline the sentence that gives the two pet sitting rates.

Cerise charges $15 per day, or $85 per week.

Step 2: Write an equation that gives Cerise's pet sitting rate for n days.

Pet sitting rate for n days = $15n$

Step 3: Write a math sentence that says the weekly rate is less than the rate for n days.

$85 < 15n$

Step 4: Solve for n.

$5.67 < n$ Divide both sides by 15.

Answer the Question

Step 5: For the weekly rate to cost less than the daily rate, Martina must hire Cerise for more than 5 days.

✏ Now try these problems.

1. Dennis charges $20 per day, or $105 per week to house sit. When does the weekly rate cost less than the daily rate?

   A The number of days is less than 5.

   B The number of days is more than 5.

   C The number of days is less than 4.

   D The number of days is more than 4.

2. Anders' monthly condo payment is $495 per month. He also pays a management company a fee of $225 per month. From June to September, the management company rents his condo out to visitors. The graph shows the rent taken in each month.

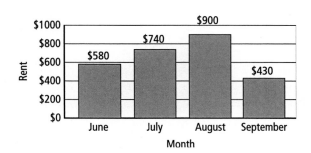

a. What is the total income from renting the condo?

Answer: The total income from renting the condo is $_____.

b. Does his condo pay for itself during the summer?

Answer: _____ (Yes/No), his condo _____ (does/does not) pay for itself.

c. How much does the management company make?

Answer: The management company makes $_____ over the four months.

3. Gail and Luce rent a condo overlooking the beach for three summer months. They each pay $350 per month. Circle the amount that is the total rent for the condo over the three month period.

$350 $700 $1,050 $2,100

4. Innis pays a real estate agent to help him sell his house. When the house sells, the agent charges him 6% of the sale price. The house sells for $56,000. Write and solve an equation to give the amount that Innis gets for the house.

Answer: _____

☆ Challenge Problem
You may want to talk this one over with a partner.

Monte is for hire as *Mr. Fix It!* In one month, he spends $450 on equipment and repairs, and earns $648 from his 'fix it' jobs. In the following month, he spends $288 on supplies, and earns $582 from his 'fix it' jobs.

a. What is the ratio of his expenses to his earnings over the two-month period?   **Answer:** _____

b. At the end of the third month, his expenses total $1,000 for the quarter. The ratio of his expenses to earnings for the quarter is equal to that of the two-month period. What were his earnings in the third month?   **Answer:** $_____

Example While Hope is traveling, she rents her home. The graph shows the income that she makes from renting her home and the income she makes from her job each season.

    a. In which season does Hope earn the most income?

    b. List the seasons of the year in order, from highest to lowest income.

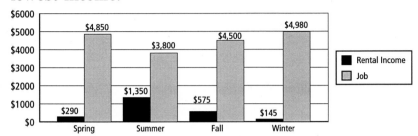

Solve

    Step 1: For each season, find Hope's income.

        Spring: $290 + $4,850 = $5,140

        Summer: $1,350 + $3,800 = $5,150

        Fall: $575 + $4,500 = $5,075

        Winter: $145 + $4,980 = $5,125

    Step 2: Now list the seasons in order, based on income: summer, spring, winter, fall

Answer the Question

    Step 3: **a.** Hope earns the most income in the summer.

             b. The seasons, in order by income, are summer, spring, winter, fall.

✏ Now try these problems.

Refer to the information in the example as you work the first problem.

   1. Hope rents out her home again, while she is traveling the next year. Each season, her rental income doubles over her rental income for the same season last year. Her income from her job stays about the same.

    a. In which season does Hope now earn the most income?

    Answer: Hope earns the most income in the _____.

    b. List the seasons of the year in order, from highest to lowest income.

    Answer: The seasons, in order by income, are _____

    _____

2. Thayne thinks he would like to rent art for his apartment. Vince shows him a table of art rental rates from the local art gallery. If

Category	Value of Art Work	Rental Fee (per month)
A	0 – $250	$9.58
B	$251 – $500	$12.83
C	$501 – $750	$14.99
D	$751 – $1,000	$19.32

Thayne pays a rental fee of $43.73 per month for four pieces of art, how many pieces does he choose and from which categories?

Answer: _____

3. Rachel searches online for rental furniture for her new apartment. One company offers complete room packages from $99.99 to $219.99 per month. She orders the 99.99 package for all three rooms. Her apartment rent is $420 per month. Which is a good estimate of what she will pay for rent and furniture each month?

    A $300   **B** $520   **C** $720   **D** $900

4. Ramiro stores other people's furniture if they let him use it. He currently has a baby grand piano, a sofa, a table and four chairs, and a refrigerator. If Ramiro rented these items, it would cost

him about $350 per month. If the owners stored these items, it would cost them about $125 per month. Circle the amount that Ramiro saves per month.

☆ *Challenge Problem*
You may want to talk this one over with a partner.

If $p + 1 = q - 2 = r + 3 = s - 4$, then which of the four quantities, p, q, r, or s, is the smallest? Explain your reasoning and the process you used.

Unit 3 — Review

Review What You Learned

In this unit you have used mathematics to solve many problems. You have used mental math and estimation, practiced basic operations, and solved equations. You have also used statistics and probability, ratios and proportions, and graphs.

These two pages give you a chance to review the mathematics you used and check your skills.

✔ Check Your Skills

1. Stafford plans to go on vacation for a week. He will leave on Friday, and come back on the following Friday. To rent a mid-size car while away, he reads the ads in his club travel magazine. What is the maximum that he can save on car rental costs?

   A
   Up to $20 OFF a Weekend or Weekly Rental!
   Weekend rentals must be for at least two days. Offer only good on mid-size or larger vehicle. You'll save $5 per day, up to $20.

   C
   $20 OFF a Car Rental In Addition to Your Club Discount!
   Rent for a minimum of five days. You'll save $20 plus your club discount.

   B
   Get Your Discount *and* Take $20 OFF any Weekly Rental!
   Rent for a minimum of five consecutive days. Offer not valid on economy cars. You'll save $20 plus your club discount.

   D
   $15 OFF! Any Car! Any Day!
   Valid for a rental of at least two days. Offer valid on any size vehicle. You'll save $15!

   Answer: _____

   If you need to review, return to lesson 1 (page 28).

2. Sawyer belongs to a movie club. The monthly charge is $15. He can download a movie whenever he wants and watch it. In one month, he downloads and watches twelve movies. The average runtime for each movie is about two hours. Which pair of answers tells the number of hours Sawyer watches movies and his cost per movie?

   A 12 hours; $1.25   **C** 12 hours; 63 cents

   B 24 hours; $1.25   **D** 24 hours; 63 cents

   If you need to review, return to lesson 2 (page 30).

38

3. Jami hires Isha to clean her apartment. Isha charges $10 per hour, or $150 per 20-hour week. When does the weekly rate cost less than the hourly rate?

Answer: _____

If you need to review, return to lesson 4 (page 34).

4. While Janel is away from home, she rents out her house. The graph shows the income that she makes from her house, and the income she makes from her job each season. List the seasons in order based on Janel's income, from highest to lowest income.

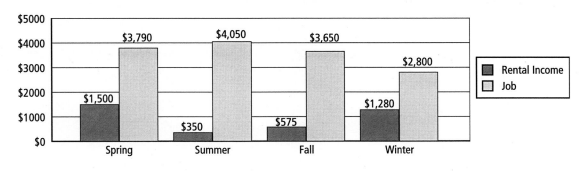

Answer: _____

If you need to review, return to lesson 5 (page 36).

Write Your Own Problem ✍️

Choose a problem you liked from this unit. Write a similar problem using a situation and related facts from your own life. With a partner, share and solve these problems together. Discuss the mathematics and compare the steps you used. If you need to, rewrite or correct the problems. Write your edited problem and the answer here.

_____

_____

_____

_____

_____

_____

_____

Preview

How You Will Use This Unit

As you think about buying on layaway, you will consider many different things. Terms and conditions, and return policies are two examples. You will probably also consider timing, and whether to buy on layaway or charge on a credit card. As you compare options and make choices, you will often use math. The math skills you use include mental math and estimation, basic operations and equations, statistics, and graphs.

What You Will Do in This Unit

In this unit, math steps demonstrate how to solve problems. These steps can help you answer questions such as these:

You buy three toys on layaway, and pay a deposit of 25% of the $80 price. If you pay the remainder in four equal installments, how much do you pay per installment?

The advertisement reads, "20% down holds anything!" You compare two music systems. One costs $450; the other costs $700. The layaway payment periods are 8 and 12 months. How do the monthly payments compare?

The sign reads, "Clearance items can be returned within 15 calendar days of purchase." You buy a skirt off the clearance rack for $15. Three weeks later you return it. What is the result of this return transaction?

In April, you buy a heavy jacket for $245 on layaway. You puts 10% down. If you want the coat by October, how much are your monthly payments?

What You Can Learn from This Unit

When you complete this unit, you will have used mathematics to work problems related to buying on layaway. These problems are similar to those that may actually occur in your daily life.

Lesson 1

→ *All Sorts of Items to Layaway*

Example Ilsa selects two Kachina dolls to buy on layaway for her collection. She pays a deposit of 25% of the total price of $80. The shop promises to hold the dolls for Ilsa for up to 90 days. Ilsa pays the remaining amount in equal installments, one installment every 30 days. If she pays the last installment on the 90th day, how much is each installment?

Solve

Step 1: Calculate the amount of money that Ilsa owes, after paying the deposit.

100% − 25% = 75%   Ilsa has 75% of the price left to pay.

75% of $80 = 0.75 × $80
            = $60

Step 2: Underline the sentence that tells how Ilsa pays the remaining amount.

<u>Ilsa pays the remaining amount in equal installments, one every 30 days.</u>

Step 3: Calculate the number of installments in 90 days.

90 ÷ 30 = 3   Divide the total number of days by the days per installments.

Step 4: Now find the amount of each installment.

$60 ÷ 3 = $20

Answer the Question

Step 5: Each installment is $20.

✎ Now try these problems.

1. Awan selects a bread-making machine for his mother. He buys it on layaway. He pays a deposit of 20% of the total price of $99. The shop will hold the bread machine for Awan for up to 60 days. Awan pays the remaining amount in equal installments, every 15 days. If he pays the last installment on the 60th day, how much is each installment? Complete the sentences to show the answer.

   Answer: Awan owes _____% of $_____ after paying the deposit.

         This is $_____.

The number of installments that Awan pays is

_____ ÷ _____ = _____.

Each installment is $_____ ÷ _____ = $_____.

2. Rusty buys a camcorder on layaway (with no down payment). Use the graph to answer the questions.

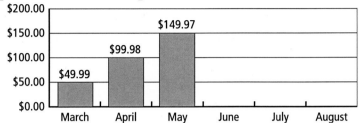

a. What does the graph show?

Answer: The graph shows _____.

b. How much is one monthly layaway payment?

Answer: One monthly layaway payment is $_____.

c. What is the total amount that Rusty pays for his camcorder?

Answer: Rusty pays $_____ for his camcorder.

3. Phoebe buys a heavy-duty sewing machine with $60 down. This down payment is 12.5% of the total cost. She pays the remainder in equal monthly installments of $42 each. How many months will it take her to pay for the machine?

Answer: _____ months

4. Marshel buys a set of tools on layaway. On the order form, Marshel reads, "Refer a friend and get paid when they start a layaway plan." Out of fifteen friends that Marshel refers, only three start layaway plans. Marshel has five more friends lined up to refer. Circle the number of these friends that the laws of probability predict will start a layaway plan. ☺ ☺ ☺ ☺ ☺

☆ *Challenge Problem*
You may want to talk this one over with a partner.

You buy a piece of furniture with a deposit of $100 and promise to pay $133 for each of the next three months. The fine print says that if you do not pay in full by the end of the 90 days, the furniture will be sold and your money forfeited. Explain the pros and cons of this layaway plan.

_____

_____

Example The advertisement in the window of the store reads: "20% down holds anything!" Rad compares two *Home Theater* systems. One costs $450; the other costs $700. The shop assistant points out the layaway plans for each system.

> **Compact Home Theater**
> Total price: $450
> 20% down
> Pay over 8 months

> **DeLux Home Theater**
> Total price: $700
> 20% down
> Pay over 12 months

  a. How do the monthly payments for the two systems compare?

  b. What is the minimum payment for either system?

  c. Draw a conclusion about the layaway time and the minimum monthly payment.

Solve

Step 1: For each system, calculate the amount remaining after the deposit is paid.

Compact Home Theater: 80% of $450 = $360
DeLux Home Theater: 80% of $700 = $560

Step 2: Calculate the monthly payment for each system over the payment period.

Compact Home Theater: $360 ÷ 8 = $45
                        Payment period is 8 months.

DeLux Home Theater: $560 ÷ 12 = $46.67
                        Payment period is 12 months.

Answer the Question

Step 3: Compare the payments for the two systems. What is the minimum monthly payment that the shop accepts for either system?

The payments are within $2 of each other. The minimum monthly payment that the shop accepts for either system is $45.

The layaway time ensures a minimum monthly payment of at least $45.

✏ Now try these problems.

Refer to the information in the example as you work through the first problem.

1. One week later, the 'Home Theater' systems are on sale. The *Compact Home Theater* system is on sale for $350, to be paid over 5 months. Rad pays 20% down and the rest per the layaway plan.

  a. What is the minimum payment that the shop accepts for the system?

Answer: The minimum monthly payment for the system is $_____.

---

b. How does this amount compare to the minimum monthly payment before the sale?

Answer: The amount is $_____ _____ (higher/lower) than before the sale.

c. Draw a conclusion about the new layaway time and minimum monthly payment.

Answer: _____

2. Kimball buys a saxophone for $480 on layaway. He wants to make minimum payments. He wonders how much sooner he will get his saxophone if he pays by credit card. Complete the equations for the time it will take him to pay by check and by credit card. Can he meet the conditions of the plan using either method of payment? Explain.

> **Layaway Terms & Conditions**
> - Payments can be made by check, credit card, or money order.
> - The first payment is at least 10% of the total purchase (or $50, if paying by credit card), and made within 10 days of the initial order.
> - Each month's payments must be at least $20 (or $50 by credit card).
> - The layaway must be complete within one year.

By check = _____ ÷ $_____ = _____ months.
(remainder after first payment)

By credit card = _____ ÷ $_____ = _____ months.
(remainder after first payment)

_____

3. At the bottom of the layaway ad, Sarah reads, "The length of the payment period depends on the amount spent." The price of one artist easel is $245, and the payment period is 8 months after a 10% down payment. Sarah notices another easel priced at $200. The payments will be about the same for both. Which expression gives the payment period for this easel, after a 10% down payment?

   A 5 months   **B** 7 months   **C** 9 months   **D** 28 months

☆ Challenge Problem
You may want to talk this one over with a partner.

You give this problem to a friend: Pick a number. Subtract 9 from that number. Divide the result by 3. However, you notice that your friend instead subtracts 3 from the number, and divides the result by 9. She tells you that her answer is 15. What answer would your friend have had if she had correctly followed your directions? Explain your steps.

_____

_____

Lesson 3

Return Policies

Example The sign above the sale rack reads, "Sale items can be returned for store credit within 15 calendar days of purchase." Non-sale items can be returned or exchanged within 30 calendar days of purchase. Layla buys a skirt off the sale rack for $15, and a jacket at the regular price of $39. Three weeks later she returns both items. What is the result of her returns?

Solve

Step 1: Underline the sentence that gives the return policy on sale items.

<u>Sale items can be returned for store credit within 15 calendar days of purchase.</u>

Step 2: What sale item did Layla buy? Did she return this item within the time stated on the sign? Does Layla get store credit for this item?

Skirt: Three weeks, or 21 calendar days, is more than the 15 days allowed.

Layla does not get store credit for this item.

Step 3: Repeat these steps for Layla's non-sale item.

<u>Non-sale items can be returned or exchanged within 30 calendar days of purchase.</u>

Jacket: 30 calendar days is more than 3 weeks (21 calendar days).

Layla can return or exchange this item.

Answer the Question

Step 4: Layla can return or exchange the jacket, but she cannot get credit for the skirt.

✐ Now try these problems.

1. The sign reads, "Sale items can be returned for store credit, within 7 calendar days of purchase." Non-sale items can be returned or exchanged within 14 calendar days of purchase. On Friday, the 3rd, Deanna buys a mountain bike off the sale rack for $95, and a helmet at the regular price of $29. On Saturday,

the 18th, she returns both items. Circle the line that shows the correct result of the return transaction.

	Mountain bike	Helmet
A	Return for store credit	Return for store credit
B	Cannot return	Return or exchange
C	Return for $\frac{4}{5}$ of the value of item	Cannot return
D	Cannot return	Cannot return

2. Javon completes his layaway payments for an outdoor camping lantern. He returns the lantern d days later. The return policy reads, "Items returned after 30 days, but before one year, will get 50% credit of the original purchase price." Which expression shows the period of time when Jason can get 50% credit back?

    A $30 < d < 365$ **C** $30 > d > 365$

    B $30 \leq d \leq 365$ **D** $30 \geq d \geq 365$

3. Joey buys a computer for $899 on layaway. He puts 10% down and starts to pay the rest in equal installments of $67.50 each. The small print says, "When a layaway plan is more than one half paid off, it cannot be discontinued. The customer can only get in-store credit for the amount paid."

    a. If Joey cannot make more than six payments, does he get an in-store credit?   **Answer:** _____ (Yes/No)

    b. If so, how much? If not, how many more payments must he make to get the credit?   **Answer: $**_____

4. In some stores, returns are subject to a 20% restocking fee. Batya returns a sofa and chairs that she originally bought on layaway for $679. What is the restocking fee? Circle the coins and bills to use and write the number of each underneath, to represent this amount.

____   ____   ____   ____   ____

☆ *Challenge Problem*
You may want to talk this one over with a partner.

How many prime numbers less than 100 have 3 as the ones digit? What are these numbers?

Lesson 4

→ *Making Payments*

♠ A Card Game (for Two or More Players)

The goal of this game is to make payments on your layaway item. First, you pick an item. Then you make payments.

Materials

Deck of item cards and deck of payment cards (on the next page)

Directions

1. Shuffle each card deck, and place face down in the center of the table. Players sit around the table.

2. In turn, each player picks a card from the *item* deck and places it face up on the table. These cards show the item each player is trying to buy.

3. Player 1 now picks a card from the *payment* card deck, and places it next to the item card. If the payment is more than the price on the item card, this player is the winner of the round. If the card is a No-More-Payments card, the player forfeits the item (and drops out of the round).

4. Players take turns picking a payment card, calculating the payment (if necessary), and comparing the payment to the item price in front of them. Each new payment card is placed alongside their other payment cards. The total is compared to the item price.

5. The round winner is the first player whose payment cards have a total that is equal (or more than) the price of the item card.

6. Discard used cards in two piles. Play the next round with the remaining cards. When the card decks are gone, shuffle each discard deck and use it again. Play as many rounds as you like.

✐ Before you play the game, try these warm-up problems.

1. Eve picks an item whose price is $120. In turn, she picks payment cards for $50, $\frac{1}{12}$ of original price, $35, and $15. How much has she paid so far?

   A $10   **B** $106   **C** $110   **D** $120

2. Palmer picks an item whose price is $360. In turn, he picks payment cards for $20, $10, and $45. The next card he picks says, "No More Payments." What does he do?

   Answer: _____

Game Cards for *Making Payments*

Make item cards for the following:

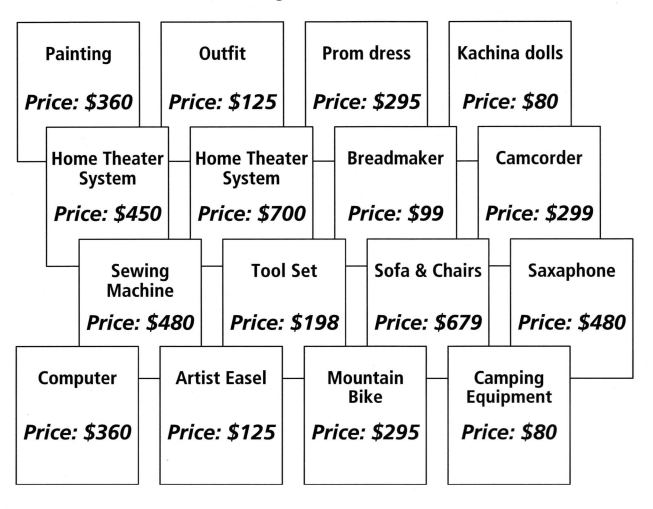

Painting *Price: $360*	**Outfit** *Price: $125*	**Prom dress** *Price: $295*	**Kachina dolls** *Price: $80*
Home Theater System *Price: $450*	**Home Theater System** *Price: $700*	**Breadmaker** *Price: $99*	**Camcorder** *Price: $299*
Sewing Machine *Price: $480*	**Tool Set** *Price: $198*	**Sofa & Chairs** *Price: $679*	**Saxaphone** *Price: $480*
Computer *Price: $360*	**Artist Easel** *Price: $125*	**Mountain Bike** *Price: $295*	**Camping Equipment** *Price: $80*

Make payment cards for the following amounts:

$10: 10 cards	$15: 10 cards
$25: 16 cards	$30: 16 cards
$40: 2 cards	$50: 2 cards

$\frac{1}{4}$ of original price: 2 cards

$\frac{1}{8}$ of original price: 4 cards

$\frac{1}{12}$ of original price: 6 cards

No More Payments: 4 cards

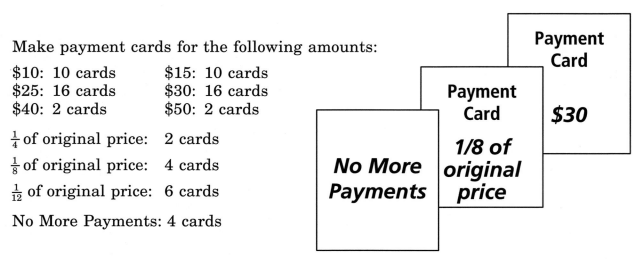

Payment Card

$30

Payment Card

1/8 of original price

No More Payments

Lesson 5

Timing Is the Key

Example: In April, Ward buys a heavy jacket for $245 on layaway. He puts 10% down. He agrees to make layaway payments of equal amounts over the six summer months. He wants the coat by the beginning of November. How much are his monthly payments?

Solve

Step 1: Calculate the amount left to pay after Ward puts 10% down.

90% of $245 = 0.9 × $245
= $220.50

Step 2: Now divide this amount by 6 to find the amount of each monthly payment.

$220.50 ÷ 6 = $36.75

Answer the Question

Step 3: Ward's monthly payments are $36.75 each.

✎ Now try these problems.

1. In July, Delle picks out a high chair for her sister, who has a new baby. Her sister tells Delle that she does not need the high chair right away. The high chair costs $135. Delle puts 15% down. She agrees to make layaway payments of $20 per month. How soon can she get the high chair?

   A July   **B** October   **C** January   **D** April

2. Devonne sees a globe that costs $96. She wonders whether to pay by credit card, or to buy the globe on layaway. She can charge the globe on her credit card and pay $20 per month. (The annual interest rate on her credit card is 12.5%.) Or she can put the globe on layaway, pay 10% down, and pay the rest over 4 months.

   a. What will each method of payment cost her per month? What is the difference?

   Answer: Paying by credit card will cost $_____ per month.

   Buying on layaway will cost $_____ per month.

   Paying by credit card will cost $_____, _____ (more/less) per month.

b. How long will it take to pay for the globe by each method? What is the difference?

Answer: It will take her ____ months by credit card, and ____ months on layaway.

Paying by credit card will take ____ month(s) _____ (more/less).

3. Weston wants a digital camera for the class reunion. One camera is on sale for $329. But he cannot buy this camera on layaway. He can buy another camera that costs $415 on layaway. He does not have $329 cash, but he has a credit card. Also, the class reunion does not happen for six months. What would you do?

Answer: _____

_____

_____

4. Petro puts $85—or one fifth—down on a painting for his new

	Payments per month	Full price of the payment
A	$68	$340
B	$68	$425
C	$85	$425

apartment. He agrees to pay the rest over 5 months. How much does he pay per month? What is the full price of the painting? Circle the row that shows the correct answers.

☆ Challenge Problem
You may want to talk this one over with a partner.

The sum of the first 25 positive even integers is 650. What is the sum of the first 25 positive odd integers? Explain the difference between the two sums.

_____

_____

_____

Unit 4 — Review

Review What You Learned

In this unit you have used mathematics to solve many problems. You have used mental math and estimation, practiced basic operations, and solved equations. You have also used statistics and graphs.

These two pages give you a chance to review the mathematics you used and check your skills.

✔ Check Your Skills

1. Yosef selects two pieces of art to buy on layaway. He pays a deposit of 25% on the total price of $120. The shop promises to hold the art for him for up to 60 days. He pays the remaining amount in equal installments, one installment every 30 days. If he pays the last installment on the 60th day, how much is each installment?

   A $15   **B** $30   **C** $45   **D** $90

   If you need to review, return to lesson 1 (page 41).

2. The advertisement on one rack in the clothing store reads, "20% down holds anything!" Ashanti compares two prom dresses. One costs $280; the other costs $600. The shop assistant points to the layaway plans for each dress. How do the monthly payments for the dresses compare? What is the minimum payment that the shop accepts per month for either dress?

Evening's Delight
Total price: $280
20% down
Pay over 6 months

Sheer Elegance
Total price: $600
20% down
Pay over 12 months

   Answer: The difference in the monthly payment is $_____.

   The minimum payment that the shop accepts for either

   dress is $_____.

   If you need to review, return to lesson 2 (page 43).

3. The sign above the sale shelf reads, "Sale items can be returned for store credit within 5 calendar days of purchase." Non-sale items can be returned or exchanged within 15 calendar days of purchase. On Thursday evening, Marcus buys an underwater camera from the sale shelf

for $115 and new fins at the regular price of $52. On the following Wednesday, he returns both items. Circle the line that represents the correct result of the return transaction.

	Camera	Fins
A	Return for store credit	Return for store credit
B	Cannot return	Return or exchange
C	Return for $\frac{4}{5}$ of the value of item	Cannot return
D	Cannot return	Cannot return

If you need to review, return to lesson 3 (page 45).

4. In October, Wyome buys a swimsuit for $85 on layaway. She puts 10% down. She agrees to make layaway payments of equal amounts over the next six months. She wants the swimsuit by the beginning of May. Complete the equation to show the amount of each monthly payment.

Answer: (_____% × $85) ÷ _____ = $_____

If you need to review, return to lesson 5 (page 49).

Write Your Own Problem ✍️

Choose a problem you liked from this unit. Write a similar problem using a situation and related facts from your own life. With a partner, share and solve these problems together. Discuss the mathematics and compare the steps you used. If you need to, rewrite or correct the problems. Write your edited problem and the answer here.

_____

_____

_____

_____

On layaway

_____

_____

_____

_____

_____

Getting the Best Deal

Preview

How You Will Use This Unit

Getting the best deal means many different things. Choosing time or place, buying on sale or in bulk are some examples. You might also consider the benefit of buying tickets for a whole season or think about the advantages of making reservations in advance. As you compare options and make choices, you will often use math. The math skills you use include mental math and estimation, basic operations and equations, statistics and probability, ratios and proportions, and graphs.

What You Will Do in This Unit

In this unit, math steps demonstrate how to solve problems. These steps can help you answer questions such as these:

An advertisement for a monthly magazine reads, "Twelve months for $4— and get two months free!" The newsstand price is $3.50. How much can you save per copy, over the newsstand price?

You and a friend compare hotel rates on a chart. You find the price of a double room at the most expensive hotel. Where could you each get a single room for that same price?

At a tradeshow, you look at the new line of printers. The cash-back offer on the $45 model is $10. There is a direct relationship between the price of a printer and the cash-back offer. What is the cash-back offer likely to be on the $80 model?

You look at a listing of foreign currency rates per dollar. You compare the rates one year ago to the rates today. You wonder on which day you will get the best exchange rate.

What You Can Learn from This Unit

When you complete this unit, you will have used mathematics to work problems related to getting the best deal. These problems are similar to those that may actually occur in your daily life.

Example Corbin reads an advertisement for a monthly travel magazine that reads, "Subscribe now and get two months free!" The newsstand price of the magazine is $3.50 per copy. The subscription rates for the magazine are shown in the table. Corbin wonders whether a one-, two-, or three-year subscription is the best deal. What is the maximum amount he can save, per copy, over the newsstand price?

Number of years	Subscription
1 year	$42
2 years	$72
3 years	$90

Solve

Step 1: For a 1-year subscription, find the price of the magazine per month.

Subscription applies to 12 months plus 2 free months.

Cost per month = $42 ÷ (12 + 2)
= $3

Step 2: Now find the price per month for the 2- and 3-year subscriptions.

2-year subscription: Cost per month = $72 ÷ (24 + 2)
= $2.77

3-year subscription: Cost per month = $90 ÷ (36 + 2)
= $2.37

Step 3: Now find the maximum amount that he can save per copy over the newsstand price.

$3.50 − $2.37 = $1.13

Answer the Question

Step 4: The maximum amount Corbin can save per copy is $1.13.

✏ Now try these problems.

1. Rawnie reads an advertisement for an adventure magazine that comes out once every two months. It reads, "Subscribe now and get two issues free!" The newsstand price of the magazine is $5.25 per copy. Complete the table to show the price per copy for a one-, two-,

or three-year subscription, including the advertisement offer. What is the maximum amount that she can save per copy, over the newsstand price?

Number of years	Subscription	Price per copy
1 year	$29.70	$_____ ÷ _____ = $_____
2 years	$54	$_____ ÷ _____ = $_____
3 years	$76.50	$_____ ÷ _____ = $_____

Answer: The maximum amount that Rawnie can save per copy

is $_____ ÷ _____ = $_____

2. Jax signs up for a new Internet service that regularly costs $19.99 per month. He gets 2 extra months free when he signs up for one year. Which expression gives the mean cost per month of this service over the year?

A $\frac{5}{6}$ of $19.99   C $\frac{7}{6}$ of $19.99

B $\frac{6}{7}$ of $19.99   D $\frac{6}{5}$ of $19.99

3. Judy watches the swimwear prices. Where is there the greatest change in the average price from one data point to the next? What is this amount?

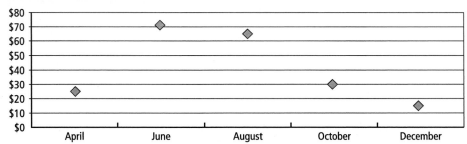

Answer: _____

☆ *Challenge Problem*
You may want to talk this one over with a partner.

You read a chart that gives the approximate value of a car as its age increases. For five consecutive years, the value of one car goes from $21,000 to $16,000 to $12,000 to $9,000 to $7,000. What do you predict the value of the car to be in the sixth year? Explain your answer.

_____

_____

♜ A Board Game (for Two or More Players)

The goal of this game is to see how long your money will last. First, you toss the number cube. Then you move your counter and calculate how much money you have left.

Materials

Game board (on the next page), a counter for each player, one number cube, and a recording sheet

Directions

1. Choose a counter color for each player. Start a new recording sheet with $500 for each player. Sit with players around the game board.

2. Each player places their counter on a different sector of the game board.

3. Player 1 tosses the number cube, and moves the counter that number of sectors around the game board. The player then does the calculation, and subtracts the result from $500. Record the result on the recording sheet.

4. Players take turns tossing the number cube, moving their counters, and calculating how much money they have left from their original $500.

5. When one player is out of money, the game is over. Who got the best deals? Compare your moves and decide!

✏ Before you play the game, try these warm-up problems.

1. On Marini's first turn, she throws a 4. She lands on a sector that says, "$15 × toss if less than 3; $10 × toss if 3 or more." How much does she spend? How much does she have left over from $500?

   A $40; $460   **C** $45; $455

   B $40; $540   **D** $45; $545

2. Locke throws a 5. He lands on a sector that says, "$75, if today's date is between the first and the 15th of the month; $60, if it is not." Today's date is March 21st. How much does Locke have left over from the $210 he still has to spend?

   Answer: $_____

Game Board for *A Matter of Timing*

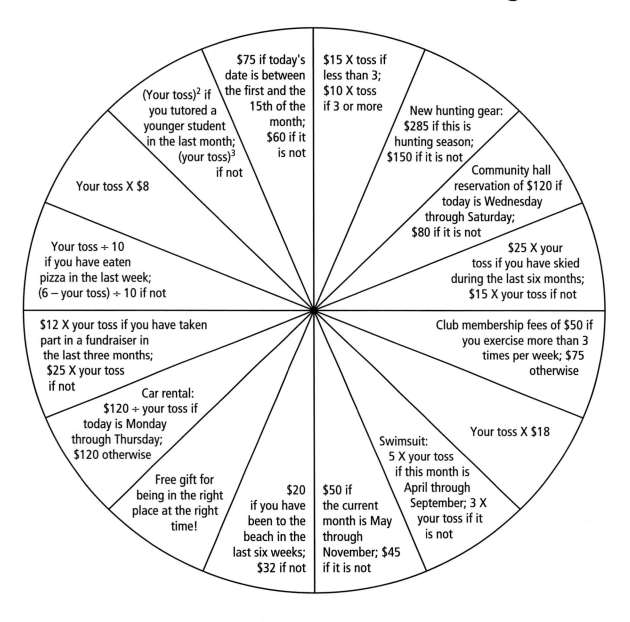

$75 if today's date is between the first and the 15th of the month; $60 if it is not

$15 X toss if less than 3; $10 X toss if 3 or more

(Your toss)^2 if you tutored a younger student in the last month; (your toss)^3 if not

New hunting gear: $285 if this is hunting season; $150 if it is not

Your toss X $8

Community hall reservation of $120 if today is Wednesday through Saturday; $80 if it is not

Your toss ÷ 10 if you have eaten pizza in the last week; (6 − your toss) ÷ 10 if not

$25 X your toss if you have skied during the last six months; $15 X your toss if not

$12 X your toss if you have taken part in a fundraiser in the last three months; $25 X your toss if not

Club membership fees of $50 if you exercise more than 3 times per week; $75 otherwise

Car rental: $120 ÷ your toss if today is Monday through Thursday; $120 otherwise

Your toss X $18

Free gift for being in the right place at the right time!

$20 if you have been to the beach in the last six weeks; $32 if not

$50 if the current month is May through November; $45 if it is not

Swimsuit: 5 X your toss if this month is April through September; 3 X your toss if it is not

Lesson 3

Vacation Deals

Example Fern and Cammi compare hotel rates. During the high season, where could they each get a single room for the price of a double room at the Palm Plaza?

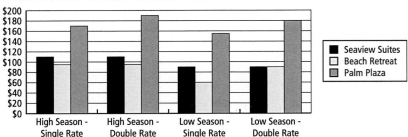

Solve

Step 1: First identify the bars on the graph that refer to the high-season rates. Then estimate from the graph the high-season single room rate at each of the three hotels.

The first two sets of three bars refer to the high-season rates.
Seaview Suites: $110
Beach Retreat: $95
Palm Plaza: $170

Step 2: Estimate the high-season double room rate at the Palm Plaza.

$190

Step 3: Compare prices to find the hotel at which two single rooms cost the same or less than the price of a double room at the Palm Plaza.

Seaview Suites: $2 \times \$110 > \$190$
Beach Retreat: $2 \times \$95 = \$190$

Answer the Question

Step 4: During high season, Fern and Cammi could each get a single room at Beach Retreat for the price of a double room at the Palm Plaza.

✏️ Now try these problems.

Refer to the information in the example as you work through the first two problems.

1. Fern and Cammi look at the low season rates.

   a. Would it be cheaper or more expensive to take two single rooms at Seaview Suites compared to a double room at Palm Plaza? By how much?

Answer: It would be _____ to take two single rooms at Seaview Suites.

b. Is the ratio of the price of a single room at Beach Retreat to the price of a double room at Palm Plaza the same during the low season as it is during the high season?

Answer: The ratio of the price of a single room at Beach Retreat to the price of a double room at Palm Plaza

is _____ during the low season.

2. The newspaper ad reads, "Save up to $106 on Thanksgiving airfares. Average peak ticket price is $391 round trip." Bron plans to depart on November 26 and return on November 30. A regular ticket would cost him $528. Complete the line that applies to his trip. Show the final price of his ticket. Show the fraction of the price of a regular ticket he saves.

Depart	Return	Average savings per ticket	Final ticket price	Fraction saved
November 25	November 26	$106		
November 26	November 29	$91		
November 25	December 1	$85		
November 26	November 30	$48		

3. Anzu pays $297 for an off-peak holiday air ticket. She says that she saved 43%. Circle the regular price of this ticket.

   $127.71 $424.71 $521.05 $690.70

☆ Challenge Problem
You may want to talk this one over with a partner.

You compare special holiday car rentals. A compact car that will carry 2 adults, 2 children, and 3 suitcases costs $20 per day. A full-size car that will carry 4 adults and 5 suitcases costs $25 per day. An SUV that carries 6 adults, 1 child, and 4 suitcases costs $35 per day. Think about a trip you have just taken or are about to take. Which is the most cost-effective deal for you? Explain your answer.

_____

_____

Lesson 4

Trade Show Opportunities

Example At a tradeshow, Jerrell looks at the line of new *Photoprint* products. The cash-back offer on the $260 *PocketPhoto* model is $100. The cash-back offer on the $180 *DesktopPhoto* model is $50. There is a direct relationship between the price of a new *Photoprint* product and the cash-back offer. This relationship is given by the general equation $Px + c = y$. P is the price of the camera, and y is the cash-back amount. What is the cash-back offer likely to be on the $340 *TurboPhoto* model?

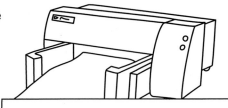

Up to $150 cash back when you buy one of our new Photoprint products today!

Solve

Step 1: Write an equation for the *PocketPhoto* model. Write a similar equation for the *DesktopPhoto* model.

$260x + c = 100$ *PocketPhoto* model
$180x + c = 50$ *DesktopPhoto* model

Step 2: Solve for x and c.

$80x = 50$ Subtract the second equation from the first.

$x = \frac{5}{8}$

$260 \times \frac{5}{8} + c = 100$ Substitute the value for x in the first equation.

$c = -\frac{500}{8}$ You can leave this fraction unreduced as you use it.

Step 3: Now write the equation for the *TurboPhoto* model. Substitute the values for x and c. Solve for the cash-back amount.

$340 \times \frac{5}{8} - \frac{500}{8} = 150$

Answer the Question

Step 4: The cash-back offer on the $340 *TurboPhoto* Model is likely to be $150.

✏ Now try these problems.

Refer to the information in the example as you work through the first problem.

1. On the same tradeshow stand as the other new *Photoprint* products, Jerrell sees a $108 *HandiPhoto* model. There is a direct

relationship between the price of a new product and the cash back offer for all *Photoprint* products. What is the cash back offer likely to be on the $108 *HandiPhoto* model?

   A $5   **C** $25   **B** $10   **D** $50

2. At one tradeshow booth, Jerrell wonders whether to put one or two of his business cards into the bowl for the drawing. There are 84 cards in the bowl when the drawing takes place. What is the probability that Jerrell will win?

   Answer: If Jerrell puts one card into the bowl, the probability of his winning is _____.

   If he puts two cards into the bowl, the probability of his winning is _____.

3. Resi wins a trip around the bay on a cruiser shown at a boat show. The trip takes a whole morning. This leaves her 4 hours to visit the 12 tradeshow booths that she is interested in. What is the average portion of the 4 hours she can give to each booth? Draw a diagram to show the answer.

4. Dacey wanders around the computer tradeshow floor. At one computer vendor's booth, he gets a 2-minute demo. He then plays with the new laptop computer for 5 minutes. At a competitor's booth, he gets a 5-minute demo, but can only play with that product for 2 minutes. In your opinion, which is the better deal? Explain your answer.

   Answer: _____

   _____

☆ Challenge Problem
You may want to talk this one over with a partner.

A tradeshow vendor offers you a puzzle that has three dials. The left dial contains the digits 2 and 3. The middle dial contains the digits 3, 4, and 7. The right dial contains the digits 5, 6, and 9. Combine the left, middle, and right digits in as many combinations as you can. How many three-digit prime numbers can you make? What are they?

_____

_____

Example Bailey is getting ready to take a trip abroad. She looks at the newspaper listing of foreign currency rates per dollar.

    a. For which currency has there been the greatest rate difference from one year ago to today, Tuesday?

    b. To get the best deal, should Bailey have bought each currency on Monday or Tuesday?

New York Rates	Tuesday	Monday	6 months ago	One year ago
British pound	0.5881	0.5906	0.6155	0.6325
Euro	0.8372	0.8499	0.8637	0.9918
Hong Kong dollar	7.7582	7.7635	7.7987	7.7991
Swiss franc	1.2941	1.3219	1.3068	1.4550

Solve

Step 1: For each currency, find the difference between the rate one year ago and today's rate.

British pound: 0.6325 − 0.5881 = 0.0444
Euro: 0.9918 − 0.8372 = 0.1546
Hong Kong dollar: 7.7991 − 7.7582 = 0.0409
Swiss franc: 1.4550 − 1.2941 = 0.1609

Step 2: For each currency, compare the currency rates for Monday and Tuesday.

	Monday		Tuesday
British pound:	0.5906	>	0.5881
Euro:	0.8499	>	0.8372
Hong Kong dollar:	7.7635	>	7.7582
Swiss franc:	1.3219	>	1.2941

Answer the Question

Step 3: a. The Swiss franc shows the greatest rate difference.

       b. Bailey should have bought all four currencies on Monday.

✎ Now try these problems.

Refer to the information in the example as you work through the first problem.

    1. Hazel looks at the same newspaper listing of foreign currency rates per dollar.

---

a. For which currency has there been the greatest rate difference from 6 months ago to yesterday, Monday? What is this difference?

Answer: The _____ shows the greatest rate difference;

the difference is _____.

b. Based on these rate differences, should Hazel have bought currency on Monday? Why?

Answer: _____

2. Jon-Michel gives Thatcher half-an-hour start in their long-distance practice race. Thatcher runs at 5 miles per hour. Jon-Michel runs at 6 miles per hour. Complete the graph to show Jon-Michel's progress against Thatcher's progress.

a. How would you interpret the graph to tell when Jon-Michel catches Thatcher?

Answer: _____

b. How does the graph tell how far apart the students are as the race progresses?

Answer: _____

3. Anais reads the ad for the gift subscription. What is the difference between the 30-week offer and the 60-week offer? What is the value of the free weeks?

Answer: _____

_____

> **Celebrate with a Gift Subscription Today!**
> 13 weeks for $39
> 30 weeks for $78
> (includes 4 weeks free)
> 60 weeks for $156
> (includes 8 weeks free)

☆ *Challenge Problem*
You may want to talk this one over with a partner.

A palindrome is a word, verse, or number that reads the same backwards as forward, such as 313 or *pop*. Start with any whole number with multiple digits. Add to it the number that is formed by reversing the digits. To this sum add the number formed by reversing the sum's digits. Continue with this process. Will you end up with a numerical palindrome? Show three examples!

Review What You Learned

In this unit you have used mathematics to solve many problems. You have used mental math and estimation, practiced basic operations, and solved equations. You have also used statistics and probability, ratios and proportions, and graphs.

These two pages give you a chance to review the mathematics you used and check your skills.

✔ Check Your Skills

1. Darryl reads an offer for a monthly sports magazine. It reads, "Subscribe now and get one month free!" The newsstand price of the magazine is $4.25 per copy. The subscription rates are below. Complete the table to show the price per copy for each subscription, including the offer. What is the maximum amount that Darryl can save per copy over the newsstand price?

Number of years	Subscription	Price per copy
1 year	$48	$_____ ÷ _____ = $_____
2 years	$84	$_____ ÷ _____ = $_____
3 years	$117	$_____ ÷ _____ = $_____

Answer: $_____

If you need to review, return to lesson 1 (page 54).

2. Chris and Malik compare hotel rates during the ski season and the summer (low) season. At which hotel is the ratio of low season rate to high season rate the greatest? Explain.

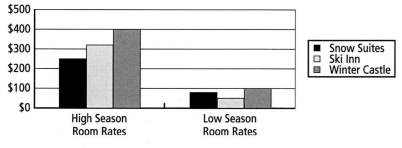

Answer: _____

_____

If you need to review, return to lesson 3 (page 58).

3. At a tradeshow, Poco looks at the new line of scooters. The cash-back offer on the $250 *Everyware* model is $80. The cash-back offer on the $350 *UpTown* model is $130. Poco hears that there is a direct relationship between the price of a new scooter and the cash-back offer. What is the cash-back offer likely to be on the $420 *StreetSmart* model?

Answer: $_____

If you need to review, return to lesson 4 (page 60).

4. Vito is getting ready to take a trip abroad. He looks at the newspaper listing of foreign currency rates per dollar. For which currency has there been the greatest rate difference from one year ago to today, Monday? What is this difference?

New York Rates	Monday	6 months ago	One year ago
British pound	0.5906	0.6155	0.6325
Euro	0.8499	0.8637	0.9918
Hong Kong dollar	7.7635	7.7987	7.7991
Swiss franc	1.3219	1.3068	1.4550

A British pound **C** Hong Kong dollar

B Euro **D** Swiss franc

The difference is _____.

If you need to review, return to lesson 5 (page 62).

Write Your Own Problem ✍

Choose a problem you liked from this unit. Write a similar problem using a situation and related facts from your own life. With a partner, share and solve these problems together. Discuss the mathematics and compare the steps you used. If you need to, rewrite or correct the problems. Write your edited problem and the answer here.

_____

_____

_____

_____

_____

Unit 6

On-line Shopping

Preview

How You Will Use This Unit

On-line shopping means many different things. Searching for a special item and keeping up-to-date on what's new are two examples. You will probably also consider making comparisons and consulting the experts. As you compare options and make choices, you will often use math. The math skills you use include mental math and estimation, basic operations and equations, statistics and probability, ratios and proportions, and graphs.

What You Will Do in This Unit

In this unit, math steps demonstrate how to solve problems. These steps can help you answer questions such as these:

You scan the Internet for tires. The minimum price for one tire is $50, and the range of the prices is $110. What is the maximum price that you could pay for this type of tire?

You search the Internet for hair products to fight frizz. You find eight with prices that range from $3.99 to $12.50. How can you estimate the mean price of these products?

In 2003, a popular drink had been on the market for 18 years. Your friend's little brother was born in 1998. How many years had the drink been on the market then?

You look at a survey in a magazine on how teens define success. On which issue is there the greatest difference of opinion between girls and boys?

What You Can Learn from This Unit

When you complete this unit, you will have used mathematics to work problems related to on-line shopping. These problems are similar to those that may actually occur in your daily life.

Lesson 1

Example Arnie scans the Internet for tires. He finds a graph that shows the price range for four tires.

a. What is the maximum price that he could pay for a tire?

b. What is the median price of a tire of this type?

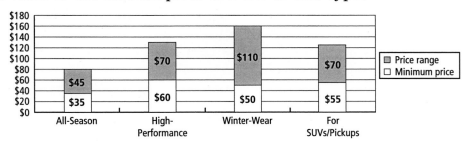

Solve

Step 1: Read the graph and all its labels. Pick the tire type with the longest bar. Now read the length of that bar off the graph.

Winter-Wear: Length of the bar is $160.

Step 2: Check your answer: write an expression for the maximum price of a tire, given the minimum price and the price range. Substitute the values for the minimum price and the price range. Check that the answer matches.

Maximum price = Minimum price + Price Range
= $50 + $110, or $160

Step 3: For this tire, write an expression and solve for the median price. The median price is the midpoint between the minimum price and the maximum price.

Winter-Wear: $\dfrac{[\$50 + (\$50 + \$110)]}{2} = \$105$

Answer the Question

Step 4: a. The maximum that Arnie could pay for a tire is $160.

b. The median price for a tire of this type is $105.

✎ Now try these problems.

Refer to the information in the example as you work the first problem.

1. Arnie looks at the graph that shows tire prices again. *Leaving out* the Winter-Wear tire, he wants to know:

---

a. What is the maximum price that he could pay for a tire?

Answer: The maximum price that he could pay for a tire is

$\$$_____.

b. What is the median price of a tire of this type? How can you determine this value from the graph?

Answer: The median price of a tire of this type is $\$$_____.

You can determine this from the graph by _____

_____.

2. Kele orders books from a used book source on the Internet that uses several different stores. Three books are advertised at $3.95, $4.85, and $6.75. For an order of less than $20, each store has a shipping charge of $5.50. Kele receives the books. Her total bill, which is correct, is $26.55. Which answer best explains the bill?

    A The total bill was less than $20, so no shipping charge was added.

    B The books were shipped from two difference stores.

    C The books were shipped from three different stores.

    D The total bill came to more than $20, so $5.50 was added.

3. Jared scans the Internet for the latest fashion colors. According to a survey, two thirds of young people between the ages of 14 and 25 adopt the latest colors immediately. There are about 1,200 young people between these ages in his community. Write an expression for the number that Meiko might expect to see in the latest colors.

Answer: _____ (fraction) × _____ (number) = _____

4. Meiko can order supplies and materials over the Internet for the race car competition. On average, he finds that the cost is 10% higher than at the local hardware store. For the items he wants, the bill at the local hardware store would be $85. Circle the amount he would pay for the same items over the Internet.

$$\$76.50 \qquad \$85.10 \qquad \$93.50 \qquad \$95.00$$

☆ Challenge Problem
You may want to talk this one over with a partner.

Imagine removing two squares of a checkerboard at opposite corners. With a domino you can take up two adjacent squares on the board. Can you completely cover this checkerboard with dominoes? Explain your answer.

_____

_____

Lesson 2

Shopping without Dropping

♜ A Board Game (for Two or More Players)

The goal of this game is to see how many moves it takes to find the item you are searching for on the Internet. First, you spin the spinner. Then you add or subtract a counter on the graph board.

Materials

Game board (on the next page), spinner (on next page), counters for each player

Directions

1. Choose a counter color for each player. Label a column for each player on the *x*-axis of the graph board. Sit with players around the game board and spinner.

2. Player 1 spins the spinner. This player then follows the directions, and adds or subtracts a counter to the bar. When a player lands on a "subtract" sector, and the result is a negative number, build the bar below the *x*-axis.

3. When a player lands on the "You found it!" sector, the round is over.

4. Players take turns and add or subtract a counter from their bar on the graph board.

5. The round winner is the first player to land on the "You found it!" sector. Discuss the results. What is each player's final position? How do the players' positions compare?

✎ Before you play the game, try these warm-up problems.

1. Casper spins the spinner and lands on "Forward three moves." He has already moved two counters in a forward direction. What is his final position on his bar?

   Answer: _____

2. Ali spins the spinner and lands on "Back two moves." He has already moved five forward and three back. What is his final position on his bar?

   A He is three forward.   **C** He is two back.

   B He is at zero.   **D** He is five back.

Spinner, Game Board for
Shopping without Dropping

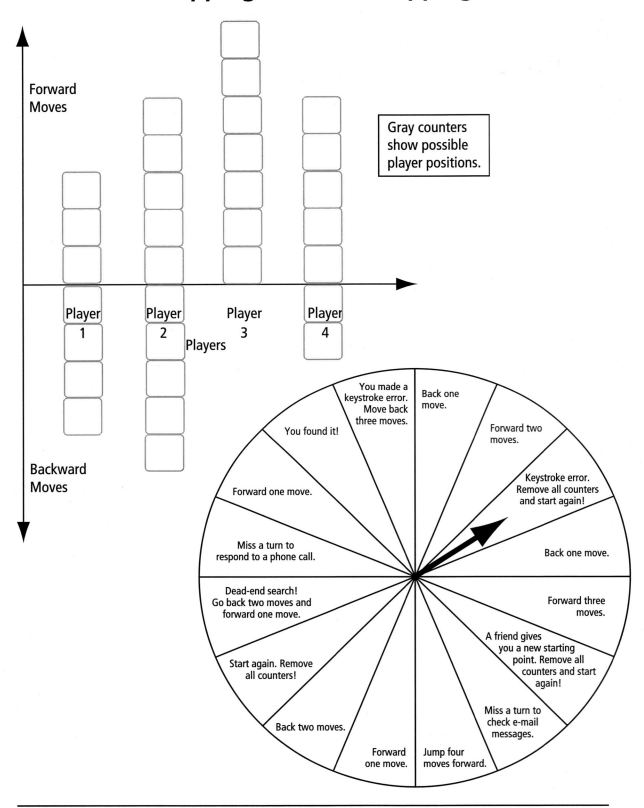

Forward
Moves

Gray counters
show possible
player positions.

Player
1

Player
2

Player
3

Player
4

Players

Backward
Moves

You made a
keystroke error.
Move back
three moves.

Back one
move.

You found it!

Forward two
moves.

Forward one move.

Keystroke error.
Remove all counters
and start again!

Miss a turn to
respond to a phone call.

Back one move.

Dead-end search!
Go back two moves and
forward one move.

Forward three
moves.

Start again. Remove
all counters!

A friend gives
you a new starting
point. Remove all
counters and start
again!

Back two moves.

Miss a turn to
check e-mail
messages.

Forward
one move.

Jump four
moves forward.

Lesson 3

Searching for Special Items

Example Howi searches the Internet and finds 40 hair products that interest her. Some control curl, some build body, and some fight frizz. All the products are priced under $25. What is a rough estimate of the mean (average) price of these products?

Number of products	3	7	7	5	7	5	4	2
Product price	$3.99	$5.19	$5.99	$6.99	$8.95	$12.50	$16.50	$21.19

Solve

Step 1: To get a rough estimate, round each price to the nearest whole number.

$3.99 → $4 $5.19 → $5 $5.99 → $6
$6.99 → $7 $8.95 → $9 $12.50 → $13
$16.50 → $17 $21.19 → $21

Step 2: Multiply these estimates by the number of products. Use the distributive property to group the products and make the mental math easier.

(3 × $4) + [7 × ($5 + $6 + $9)] + [5 × ($7 + $13)] + (4 × $17) + (2 × $21)

= $12 + $140 + $100 + $68 + $42

= $362

Step 3: Round this total to the nearest 10. Then divide by the total number of products to find the approximate mean.

$362 → $360 $360 ÷ 40 = $9

Answer the Question

Step 4: A rough estimate of the mean (average) price of these products is $9.

✏️ Now try these problems.

1. Ashland searches the Internet for hair products to fight frizz. She finds seven products. Two products cost $3.99 each, one product costs $5.19, three products cost $5.99, and one product

costs $8.95. What is a rough estimate of the mean price of these products?

Answer: A rough estimate of the mean price of the products is $____.

2. Noel spends two hours on the Internet, searching for a gift for his girlfriend. Finally he decides on two items, a jacket and a pair of earrings. The jacket costs $125.99, and the earrings cost $21.50. Which describes the rate of spending for his time?

    A $7.37 per minute   **C** $73.75 per hour

    B $14.75 per minute   **D** $147.49 per hour

3. Zena's microwave oven has stopped working. She looks for a replacement. On the Internet she finds a Web site for appliance repair. For $11.99, she can call a technician. The technician will help diagnose the problem, order parts, and talk her through the repair. All that Zena needs is a part that costs $4.99. Having a service technician come to her apartment would have cost about $65. Roughly how much does Zena save? Write an expression for this amount.

Answer: _____ = $_____

☆ *Challenge Problem*
You may want to talk this one over with a partner.

Three friends form a line that is perpendicular to a wall. Each friend stands facing the wall. You ask them to close their eyes. From a barrel of three red hats and two purple hats, you place one hat on each of your friends. Then you ask them to open their eyes but stay in line. You tell each one to guess what color hat they are wearing. The friend who is farthest from the wall sees the other two friends, and says she doesn't know. The second friend hears this reply, sees the friend ahead of her, and says she doesn't know. The friend closest to the wall hears both replies, and says she knows. What color is her hat? Explain how she knows.

_____

_____

_____

_____

_____

Lesson 4

What's New?

Example Eden scanned the Internet for interesting events. She found that in March of 2002 tennis star Jennifer Capriati was 26 years old. Eden's older sister was born in March 1979. Was Jennifer Capriati born before or after Eden's older sister? By how much?

Solve

Step 1: Draw a number line. Mark the years 2002 and 1979 on the line.

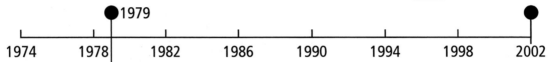

Step 2: Now count 26 years back from 2002 and make a mark on the line.

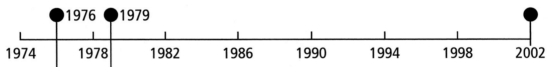

Step 3: Find the difference between when Eden's older sister was born and when Jennifer Capriati was born.

1979 − 1976 = 3

Answer the Question

Step 4: Jennifer Capriati was born before Eden's older sister by 3 years.

✎ Now try these problems.

1. In February 2003, movie star and teen rebel James Dean would have been 72 years old. Shannon's grandfather was born in February 1936. Was Shannon's grandfather born before or after James Dean? By how much?

   Answer: Shannon's grandfather was born _____ (before/after)

   James Dean, by _____ years.

2. 2003 was the year of the 75th annual *Oscar* awards. In what year did the first event occur? Draw and label a diagram to show the year.

3. Jeb's school posts various anniversaries on their Web site. In 2000, the school celebrated 25 years of competitive athletics. In 2001, it celebrated 10 years of competitive softball. In 2002, it celebrated 15 years of competitive basketball. And in 2003, it celebrated 5 years of competitive tennis. What was the *first* year in which the school competed in each of these sports? Match a date to a sport by drawing a line to show the answers.

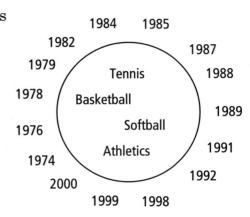

4. Danice follows the surfing news on a teen Web site. This month the Web site highlights four top female surfers who are competing in an upcoming competition for a major prize. There are 20 other competitors registered for the competition. All of the 24 competitors have won a major surfing competition in the last few meets. What is the probability that one of the four in the news will win the prize?

    A $\frac{1}{24}$ **B** $\frac{1}{20}$ **C** $\frac{1}{6}$ **D** $\frac{1}{5}$

☆ *Challenge Problem*
You may want to talk this one over with a partner.

If $a - 1 = b + 2 = c - 3 = d + 4$, which of a, b, c, or d, is the smallest? Explain how you got your answer.

_____

_____

_____

_____

_____

Example Slade looks at a survey on the Internet about how teens define success. On which key is there the greatest difference of opinion? What is this difference?

Keys to Success	Girls	Boys
Doing something you love, no matter how much money you make	61%	61%
Making lots of money	17%	24%
Seeing oneself as an equal breadwinner	77%	42%
Being happily married	6%	6%

Solve

Step 1: Select the keys to success where there is a difference of opinion.

Keys to Success	Girls	Boys
Making lots of money	17%	24%
Seeing oneself as an equal breadwinner	77%	42%

Step 2: Compare the percent ratings for these keys to success.

Making lots of money: $24\% - 17\% = 7\%$

Seeing oneself as an equal breadwinner: $77\% - 42\% = 35\%$

Answer the Question

Step 3: The greatest difference of opinion is in seeing oneself as an equal breadwinner. On this, 35% more girls than boys choose the key of seeing themselves as an equal breadwinner.

✎ Now try these problems.

Refer to the information in the example as you work the second problem.

1. Sharie conducts a similar survey over the high school network. On which key is there the greatest difference of opinion? By how much?

Keys to Success	Girls	Boys
Making lots of money	32%	49%
Seeing oneself as an equal breadwinner	80%	65%

Answer: _____

2. Whitney finds that 342 out of 855 girls and 273 out of 455 boys at her school believe that making lots of money is a key to success.

    a. Write an equation for the percent of girls and percent of boys at her school who believe this is so.

Answer: Girls: _____ = ____%

              Boys: _____ = ____%

    b. Do her figures match the Internet survey figures? What is the difference?

Answer: Her figures _____ (do/do not) match the survey figures.

                _____% _____ (more/less) girls in Whitney's survey believe that making lots of money is a key to success.

                _____% _____ (more/less) boys in Whitney's survey believe that making lots of money is a key to success.

3. Adrian finds the results of a teen survey on the Internet. A graph of the survey results shows what teens think will be achieved in their lifetimes.

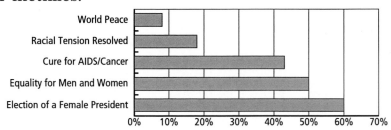

    a. Approximately how many more teens believe that a cure for AIDS/cancer will be found than world peace?

Answer: _____%

    b. Which events do more than 40% of the teens surveyed believe will happen? Explain.

Answer: _____

☆ *Challenge Problem*
You may want to talk this one over with a partner.

You pay $72 for a camera on sale. You want to offer it for sale on the Internet with a 10% discount on its list price. You also want to make a profit of 25% on the price you paid. Write and solve an equation to find the price that you put on the camera.

_____

Review What You Learned

In this unit you have used mathematics to solve many problems. You have used mental math and estimation, practiced basic operations, and solved equations. You have also used statistics and probability, ratios and proportions, and graphs.

These two pages give you a chance to review the mathematics you used and check your skills.

✔ Check Your Skills

1. Paula scans the Internet and finds a graph that shows the price range for three tires.

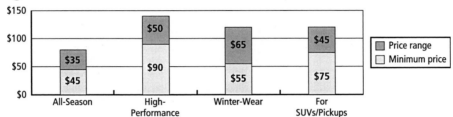

   a. What is the maximum price that she could pay for a tire?

   Answer: $_____

   b. Write equations to find the median prices of a Winter-Wear tire and of a tire for SUVs/Pickups. What is the difference in these prices?

   Answer: Winter-Wear: _____

   For SUVs/Pickups: _____

   The difference is $_____

   If you need to review, return to lesson 2 (page 69).

2. Ciddie searches the Internet for hair products that build body. She finds eight that are under $15. Prices range from $3.99 to $12.50. Write an expression to make a rough estimate of the mean price of these products.

Number of products	1	2	2	2	1
Product price	$3.99	$5.19	$5.99	$8.95	$12.50

   Answer: _____ = $_____

   If you need to review, return to lesson 3 (page 71).

3. The Girl Scouts of America began in 1912. Maria's grandmother celebrated her 80th birthday in 2002. Did the Girl Scouts already exist when she was born? By how many years did the two events miss each other? Draw a diagram to show the answer.

If you need to review, return to lesson 4 (page 73).

4. Alexis looks at a survey on the Internet about how teens see themselves. Circle the issue for which there is the greatest difference of opinion. To the right of this issue, write the difference between the girls' and boys' percents.

Health & Looks	Girls	Boys
Comfortable with one's body	41%	56%
Concerned about weight	39%	28%
Concerned about fitness	19%	31%

If you need to review, return to lesson 5 (page 75).

Write Your Own Problem ✍️

Choose a problem you liked from this unit. Write a similar problem using a situation and related facts from your own life. With a partner, share and solve these problems together. Discuss the mathematics and compare the steps you used. If you need to, rewrite or correct the problems. Write your edited problem and the answer here.

Unit 7

Shopping for a Neighbor

Preview

How You Will Use This Unit

Shopping for a neighbor means many different things. Knowing how they think and following their lists are two examples. You will probably also consider whether to buy recognized brands or generic brands. You may also think about what quantities to buy. As you compare options and make choices, you will often use math. The math skills you use include mental math and estimation, basic operations and equations, statistics and probability, ratios and proportions, and graphs.

What You Will Do in This Unit

In this unit, math steps demonstrate how to solve problems. These steps can help you answer questions such as these:

You shop for a neighbor who has allergies. Four out of five things that you can eat, your neighbor cannot eat. You pick a can off the shelf without looking at the label. What is the probability that your neighbor cannot eat the contents?

You visit a friend's neighbor. The neighbor has a long list of things to pick up in town. You look at a map and calculate distances to find out the distance for the round trip.

You and a neighbor combine shopping so that you can save by buying in volume. The checkout screen shows that you save $1 when you buy one item, and $10 when you buy 5 items. How much would you save if you buy 100 items?

You find an Internet site that promotes shopping for a neighbor. Your first "neighbor" lives 45 minutes away. Shopping takes about $3\frac{1}{4}$ hours. How many hours does this take out of your day?

What You Can Learn from This Unit

When you complete this unit, you will have used mathematics to work problems related to shopping for a neighbor. These problems are similar to those that may actually occur in your daily life.

Lesson 1

Example Lyn regularly shops for his neighbor. His neighbor has a long list of allergies. Lyn knows that four out of five things that he, Lyn, can eat, his neighbor cannot eat. Lyn picks a can of food off the supermarket shelf, without looking at the label. What is the theoretical probability that his neighbor cannot eat the contents?

Salmon Chowder

Solve

Step 1: Underline the sentence that tells what Lyn's neighbor can eat.

Lyn knows that four out of five things that he, Lyn, can eat, his neighbor cannot eat.

Step 2: Out of five cans of food, how many cans contain something that Lyn's neighbor can probably not eat?

4 out of 5   This is the favorable outcome.

Step 3: Write the total number of possible outcomes.

5 out of 5

Step 4: Now write the probability as the fraction of favorable outcomes to possible outcomes.

$\frac{4}{5}$

Answer the Question

Step 5: The probability that Lyn's neighbor cannot eat the contents is $\frac{4}{5}$.

✏️ Now try these problems.

1. Trella is shopping for her neighbor. She recalls that this neighbor dislikes most green vegetables. Three out of four green vegetables her neighbor will not eat. Trella picks out broccoli. What is the theoretical probability that her neighbor will eat it?

   A $\frac{1}{4}$ B $\frac{3}{7}$ C $\frac{4}{7}$ D $\frac{3}{4}$

2. Val's house-bound neighbor prefers house brands to brand-name products. Out of eight hair-care products, two are house brands. There are 4 kinds of vitamin C. If the same ratio holds true for

the vitamin C products, how many are house brands? Write an equation for the answer.

Answer: Number of house brand vitamin C products:

_____ ÷ _____ × _____ = _____

3. Vienna's neighbor loves historical fiction novels. Vienna goes to this year's library book sale. She picks out several books for her neighbor. She lists the book-sale price and an estimate of the regular bookstore price. Complete the table to show how much her neighbor saves over the bookstore price.

Book	Book-sale price	Regular price	Estimated savings
One new release	$4	$21 each	
Three hardbacks	75 cents each	$15 each	
5 paperbacks	25 cents each	$5 each	
10 *History-in-Fiction* magazines	$3 total	$2 each	
TOTAL SAVINGS			

4. Tin's neighbor considers three-fifths of the foods on the ethnic-food isle of the supermarket to be luxury items. There are 375 different items on that aisle. How many would Tin's neighbor consider to be luxuries?

Answer: _____

☆ *Challenge Problem*
You may want to talk this one over with a partner.

You toss a number cube five times. What is the theoretical probability of tossing a 6 each time? Explain how you got your answer.

_____

_____

_____

_____

_____

_____

Example When Erik visits his father, he often stops by and visits his father's downstairs neighbor. On this trip, his father's neighbor has a long list of things to pick up in town. Eric offers to pick them up. The neighbor gives him a map. He tells Erik that all streets are at right angles to each other. How far is the round trip?

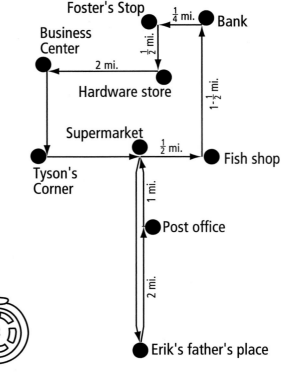

Solve

Step 1: Start at Erik's father's place and check the route. List any unknown distances.

Business center to Tyson's Corner and Tyson's Corner to the Supermarket

Step 2: Analyze the map and calculate these distances.

Business center to Tyson's Corner = (Fish Shop to Bank) − (Foster's Stop to Hardware store) = $(1\frac{1}{2} - 1)$ miles

Tyson's Corner to the Supermarket = (Bank to Foster's Stop) + (Hardware store to Business Center) − (Supermarket to Fish shop) = $(\frac{1}{4} + 2 - \frac{1}{2})$ miles

Step 3: Add the mileage as you follow the arrows around the route.

$(2 + 1 + \frac{1}{2} + 1\frac{1}{2} + \frac{1}{4} + \frac{1}{2} + 2 + 1 + 1\frac{3}{4} + 1 + 2)$ miles = $13\frac{1}{2}$ miles

Answer the Question

Step 4: The round trip is $13\frac{1}{2}$ miles.

✏️ Now try these problems.

Refer to the information in the Example as you work the first problem.

1. One month later, Erik visits his father again. He again shops for his father's downstairs neighbor. This time he does not have to go to the bank or Foster's Stop.

   a. List the distances for each segment of this round trip.

   Answer: _____ miles

   b. How much shorter is this round trip?

   Answer: This round trip is _____ mile shorter.

2. Chris's roommate breaks her arm playing basketball. Chris gives her a hand organizing her things. It takes 40 minutes to pick up all the books. It takes an hour to fold and put away the clean wash. It takes half an hour to make a list of things her roommate needs to do. Her roommate says she owes Chris all this time back. But Chris says, "Half of the books belong to me, so only count half of that time." How much time does Chris's roommate owe her?

   A 51 minutes   **C** 1 hour 50 minutes

   B 1 hour 5 minutes   **D** 2 hours 10 minutes

3. Kamilla's neighbor gives Kamilla a list of items to buy at a local co-op food store. The neighbor notes what she expects to pay. Kamilla adds to the table the price that she would regularly pay. Complete the table to show how much her neighbor saves over the regular price.

Item	Co-op-food price	Regular price	Savings
$\frac{1}{2}$ pound of mozzarella cheese	50 cents per pound	$5.75 per pound	
2 pounds of cheddar cheese	75 cents per pound	$4.85 per pound	
3 bags of potato chips	33 cents per bag	$1.39 per bag	
30 unlabeled cans of soup	10 cents each	65 cents each	
TOTAL SAVINGS			

☆ *Challenge Problem*
You may want to talk this one over with a partner.

Look at these four shapes. How many regular polygons can you make by putting them together?

Answer: _____

Lesson 3

Price or Quantity

Example On the checkout-counter screen, Elki sees how much she saves when she buys in volume. Elki buys what her neighbor needs. Then she adds what she needs, so that they can save on volume. How much would Elki pay for 100 items, without the volume saving plan?

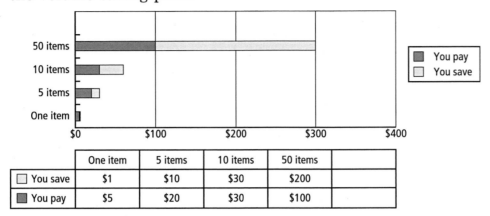

	One item	5 items	10 items	50 items	
☐ You save	$1	$10	$30	$200	
▨ You pay	$5	$20	$30	$100	

Solve

Step 1: Calculate how much Elki would pay if she paid

One item	5 items	10 items	50 items
$1 + $5 = $6	$10 + $20 = $30	$30 + $30 = $60	$200 + $100 = $300

full price for each quantity.

Step 2: Look for a pattern.

$6 = 1 × $6 $30 = 5 × $6
$60 = 10 × $6 $300 = 50 × $6

Pattern: Multiply the number of items by the full price for one item.

Step 3: Deduce how much 100 items would cost.

100 × $6 = $600

Answer the Question

Step 4: Elki would pay $600 for 100 items.

✎ Now try these problems.

Refer to the information in the example as you work the first two problems.

1. Elki wonders why the store does not advertise a volume savings plan for 100 items. What would she save if she bought 100 items with the volume saving plan? Work through the steps to find the answer.

a. Write an expression for the volume saving on each quantity.

1 × ___ = $1   5 × ___ = $10   10 × ___ = $30   50 × ___ = $200

b. Describe the pattern. _____

c. Write an expression for the volume savings on 100 items, using this information. _____

d. Why do you think the store might not advertise a volume savings plan for 100 items?_____

2. Elki buys 50 items.
   a. How much does she pay per item?

   Answer: Elki pays $_____ per item when she buys 50 items.

   b. What is the per-item price difference between buying one item and 50 items?

   Answer: The per-item price difference is $_____.

3. Filip's neighbor loves bargains. He can store cartons of his bargains under his bed. But the cartons stored there can't take up more than 2 feet by 5 feet by 6 feet. Filip sees a bargain on cans of mixed fruit. One carton of cans is 18 inches by 12 inches by 8 inches. Draw a diagram to show the maximum number of cartons that Filip's neighbor can store under his bed.

☆ *Challenge Problem*
You may want to talk this one over with a partner.

The number of petals on certain flowers increases according to a pattern. Lilies and irises have 3 petals. Buttercups and columbines have 5 petals. Delphiniums have 8 petals. Corn marigolds have 13 petals. Asters have 21 petals. Daisies have petals that take the next two numbers in this sequence. What are these two numbers? Explain how you got your answer.

Answer: The numbers are: _____ and _____.

Lesson 4

Being a Good Neighbor

Example Wendi finds an Internet site that promotes shopping for a neighbor. Her first "neighbor" lives 45 minutes away. She downloads the shopping list and leaves. At a nearby shopping mall she picks up all the items. This takes her about three and one quarter hours. She delivers everything and is home again by 6:45 p.m. Approximately how many hours does this take out of her day? When did she leave home?

Solve

Step 1: Underline the sentences that tell how long each part of the trip takes.

Her first "neighbor" lives 45 minutes away. ... This takes her about three and one quarter hours.

Step 2: Add to find the total length of the trip.

(45 minutes × 2) + $3\frac{1}{4}$ hours = $1\frac{1}{2}$ hours + $3\frac{1}{4}$ hours
= $4\frac{3}{4}$ hours

Step 3: Write a sentence that tells when she left home. Then calculate that time.

$4\frac{3}{4}$ hours before 6:45 p.m.

$6\frac{3}{4} - 4\frac{3}{4} = 2$ Convert both numbers to the same units.

Answer the Question

Step 4: Helping a neighbor takes Wendi $4\frac{3}{4}$ hours. She left home at 2 p.m.

✏️ Now try these problems.

1. Wendi tells Zea about a neat Internet site that promotes shopping for a neighbor. Zea's first "neighbor" lives one hour away. She downloads the shopping list and leaves home at about 1:30 p.m. Shopping takes her about two and one half hours. She delivers everything. Then she stops by a friend's place for an hour on the way home. Use a number line to explain when she gets home.

2. Regan needs to be at the ball game by 2:30 p.m. But he needs to pick up car parts to fix his neighbor's car before that. And he wants to stop by a dealership to look at a car his friend has mentioned. The trip will take him about three hours, plus half an hour to check out the car. What is the latest time that he can leave home, do everything, and make the game?

Answer: _____

3. Whenever Seth goes up to the mountains, he brings back something for his elderly neighbor. This time, he finds a hunter's cap to add to his neighbor's collection. The cap costs $7.95 plus 8.65% sales tax. How much does Seth pay for the cap?

    A $7.95   **C** $8.82

    B $8.64   **D** $14.83

4. When Bennie brings back her neighbor's shopping, she usually stops and visits. Her neighbor comments on the length of time that Bennie stops. She says that it is in proportion to the length of the shopping list! Usually Bennie stops for about 20 minutes. Today the list is about one and a half times as long as usual. Write an expression and find the length of time that her neighbor expects Bennie to stop.

Answer: _____ = _____

☆ *Challenge Problem*
You may want to talk this one over with a partner.

You take your neighbor's car to a car wash. You can pay $7.50 for a wash, vacuum, and polish. Or you can buy a discount coupon. The discount coupon gives you one wash, vacuum, and polish a week for four weeks for $20. What would you do? Explain your answer.

_____

_____

_____

_____

Lesson 5

♠ A Card Game (for Two or More Players)

The goal of this game is to complete the open ends of a *Match It!* card. First, you pick a *Match It!* card. Then you match each open end with a value card.

Materials

Match It! and value card decks (on the next page)

Directions

1. Shuffle both card decks. Place the *Match It!* card deck face down in the center of the table. Turn the top *Match It!* card up. Deal seven value cards to each player. Place the spare value cards face down in the center of the table. Sit with players around the table.

2. Player 1 compares his or her value cards with the open ends of the *Match It!* card. If there is a match, Player 1 closes the open end by placing the value card next to that open end. If no match, Player 1 doesn't make a move. Player 1 replaces the card played with one from the spare value card deck.

3. Player 2 then takes a turn matching value cards with the *Match It!* card.

4. Players take turns matching their value cards to the *Match It!* card. A round is over when a *Match It!* card is completely closed. The *Match It!* card and attached value cards are then placed face up on discard stacks. When all spare value cards are gone, the discard value stack is shuffled and used.

5. The game continues as long as players choose to play. For more complicated rounds, players can play two or more *Match It!* cards at once.

✐ Before you play the game, try these warm-up problems.

1. Teresa has a value card that reads, "$144 \div 9$." On the 15 *Match It!* card, where can she place her value card?

   Answer: _____

2. Matthew has a value card that reads, "$51 \div 3$." All open ends (except the =) on the 15 *Match It!* card are closed. What can he do with this value card?

   A Wait for another *Match It!* card.

   B Discard the *value* card.

   C Replace an existing value card.

   D Play the value card in another spot.

Cards for *Match It!*

Match It! cards:

Make *Match It!* cards for all numbers from 10 through 25, following the model for 15.

$$\begin{array}{c} 15 \\ >\quad <15 \quad =15 \quad >15 \quad < \end{array}$$

Value cards:

Make value cards with answers from 5 through 30. The set below gives one of each. Add two more cards for each number from 10 through 25. (Copy this set or make new ones!)

$20 - 7$	$39 - 32$	$63 - 39$	$73 - 53$
$36 \div 3$	$255 \div 17$	$144 \div 9$	$38 \div 2$
2×7	2×4	$69 \div 3$	6×3
$6 + 5$	$16 + 11$	$19 + 7$	$29 - 19$
$11 + 19$	7×4	$14 + 7$	$4 + 5$
$12 + 13$	$145 \div 5$	$13 - 7$	$150 \div 30$
11×2	$51 \div 3$		

Unit 7

Review

Review What You Learned

In this unit you have used mathematics to solve many problems. You have used mental math and estimation, practiced basic operations, and solved equations. You have also used statistics and probability, ratios and proportions, and graphs.

These two pages give you a chance to review the mathematics you used and check your skills.

✔ Check Your Skills

1. Del is shopping for his neighbor. He recalls that this neighbor dislikes most cereals. In fact, five out of six types of cereal that Del would choose, his neighbor will not eat. Del chooses one box of cereal. What is the theoretical probability that his neighbor will like it?

    Answer: _____

    If you need to review, return to lesson 1 (page 80).

2. When Lacey visits her sister, she often stops by and visits an elderly neighbor. On this trip, the neighbor has a long list of things to pick up in town. Lacey offers to pick them up. The neighbor gives her a map. He tells Lacey that it is only 1 mile to the hardware store. He also says that all the streets are at right angles to each other.

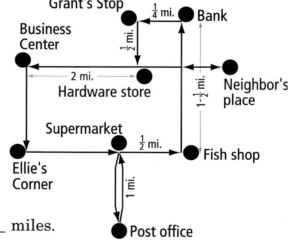

    a. How long is the round trip?

    Answer: The round trip is _____ miles.

    b. If Lacey only had to go to the Fish shop, the Bank, and the Hardware store, how long would the round trip be?

    Answer: If Lacey only had to go to the Fish shop, the Bank, and

    the Hardware store, the round trip would be _____ miles.

    If you need to review, return to lesson 2 (page 82).

3. On the checkout counter screen, Trey sees how much he saves when he buys in volume. Trey buys what his neighbor needs.

Unit 7 • Shopping for a Neighbor   **90**   © Saddleback Educational Publishing • Smart Shopping

Then he adds more, so that they can save on volume. Complete the table to show how much Trey would pay and save for 100 items. Look for a pattern in how much you save per item.

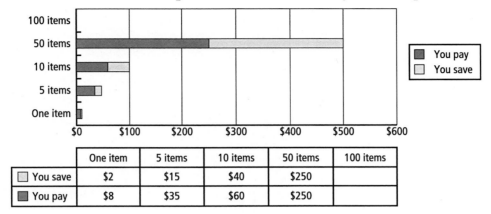

	One item	5 items	10 items	50 items	100 items
☐ You save	$2	$15	$40	$250	
■ You pay	$8	$35	$60	$250	

If you need to review, return to lesson 3 (page 84).

4. Cori finds an Internet site that promotes shopping for a neighbor. His first "neighbor" lives 30 minutes away. He downloads the shopping list and picks up all the items on the way. Shopping takes him about two and one half hours. He delivers everything and is home again by 5:30 p.m. Approximately how many hours does this take out of his day?

Answer: _____ hours

If you need to review, return to lesson 4 (page 86).

Write Your Own Problem ✍

Choose a problem you liked from this unit. Write a similar problem using a situation and related facts from your own life. With a partner, share and solve these problems together. Discuss the mathematics and compare the steps you used. If you need to, rewrite or correct the problems. Write your edited problem and the answer here.

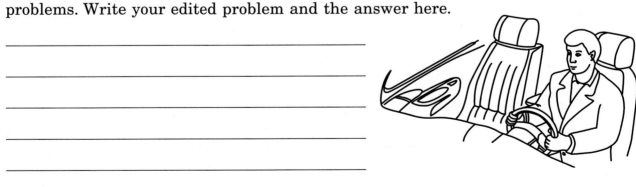

_____

_____

_____

_____

_____

_____

Preview

How You Will Use This Unit

The second time around means many different things. Buying items at garage sales and estate sales are two examples. You will probably also consider buying used books, clothes, cards, and furniture. You may also think about recycling trash. As you compare options and make choices, you will often use math. The math skills you use include mental math and estimation, basic operations and equations, statistics and probability, ratios and proportions, and graphs.

What You Will Do in This Unit

In this unit, math steps demonstrate how to solve problems. These steps can help you answer questions such as these:

You hold a yard sale on four different days for three weeks. You plot a graph to show items sold each day. If you drop one day out of the four, which day should it be?

In an estate sale, you buy three wicker chairs for $20 each. After six months, you sell them for $35 each. How much money do you make? What is your percent profit?

You buy two second-hand cars for a total of $600. You sell one of them right away for $800. One year later, you sell the second car for $400, and buy a third car for $700. How much has it cost you to own three cars?

You cut eight circles out of different greeting cards. You fold each circle so that it creates a triangle. You glue the circles together along the side folds. How many triangular faces and side folds does your figure have?

What You Can Learn from This Unit

When you complete this unit, you will have used mathematics to work problems related to the second time around. These problems are similar to those that may actually occur in your daily life.

Lesson 1

Garage Sales

Example The Booster Club holds a garage sale on four different days for three weeks to raise funds. They plot the number of items they sell on each of the four days.

a. Which day of the week was the peak selling day each week?

b. If they drop one day out of the four, which day should they drop, and why?

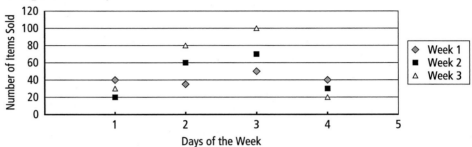

Solve

Step 1: Analyze the graph for the peak selling day each week.

Week 1 → Day 3
Week 2 → Day 3
Week 3 → Day 3

Step 2: Analyze the trend from week to week on one particular day.

Day 1 → Sales start high. Sales drop in week 2, but build back in week 3.
Days 2 and 3 → Sales build from week to week.
Day 4→ Sales drop from week to week.

Step 3: What other factor can you use to make a decision about which day to drop?

Total sales for each of the four days, over the three week period.

Answer the Question

Step 4: a. The peak selling day each week is day 3.
b. They should drop day 4, because sales drop from week to week on day 4. Also sales on day 4 (and day 1) are lower than on the other days.

✎ Now try these problems.

Refer to the information in the example as you work the first two problems.

1. The Booster Club looks at the graph for a consistent pattern. From week to week, which day is the worst selling day?

Answer: The worst selling day during week 1 is day ____.

The worst selling day during week 2 is day ____.

The worst selling day during week 3 is day ____.

2. The Booster Club continues to analyze the graph.

   a. When did they sell the most items? Match the number of items sold to the week.

Week Number	Number of Items Sold
1	180
2	230
3	165

   b. Use this information to compete the statement about the trend in popularity.

   Answer: The popularity of the garage sale is _____ (increasing/decreasing/staying the same).

3. Vivienne has been looking for a glass coffee pot to replace the one she broke. She can buy a new one for $12. But she finds one at a garage sale for $1.50. What percent of the price of a new coffee pot does she pay for her garage sale pot?

   Answer: _____%

4. Fulton buys a guitar at a garage sale for $15. Three months later, he sells the guitar for twice the price that he paid for it. How much money does he make per month?

   A $5   **B** $10   **C** $15   **D** $30

☆ *Challenge Problem*
You may want to talk this one over with a partner.

You find an old framed picture in your grandparents' attic. Your grandmother tells you that they picked it up at a garage sale on her 65th birthday. You are 70 years younger than your grandmother. You are now 17 years old. Write an equation for the number of years ago that your grandparents picked up the picture.

Answer: _____ = _____ years ago.

Lesson 2

Estate & Other Sales

Example At an estate sale, Eaton buys three wicker chairs for $20 each. After six months, he decides that he doesn't like them. He sells them for $35 each.

    a. How much money does he make?

    b. What is the percent profit on each chair?

Solve

Step 1: Underline the sentence that tells the amount of money he pays for each chair. Then underline the sentence that tells how much he sells them for.

At an estate sale, Eaton buys three wicker chairs for $20 each.

He sells them for $35 each.

Step 2: Find the difference between what he pays and the sales price of the chairs.

Per chair → $35 − $20 = $15

For all three chairs → $15 × 3 = $45

Step 3: Now calculate the percent profit on each chair.

($15 ÷ $20) × 100% = 75%

Answer the Question

Step 4: a. Eaton makes $45.

        b. His percent profit is 75% on each chair.

✏ Now try these problems.

1. At an estate sale, D'Anne buys four pieces of jewelry for $15 per piece. After a month, she decides that she doesn't like any of it. She sells it for $25 per piece.

a. How much money does she make?

Answer: She makes $_____.

b. What is the percent profit on each piece?

Answer: The percent profit on each piece is _____%.

2. Dion buys a set of three end tables at an estate sale. He estimates that the value of the smallest table is one quarter of

---

© Saddleback Educational Publishing • Smart Shopping   **95**   Unit 8 • Second Time Around the value of the set. He fixes them up and sells the smallest table for the price he paid for all three. What is his percent profit on this table?

A 8.3% **B** 25% **C** 30% **D** 300%

3. At an auction, a computer keeps track of the opening and closing bids on each item.

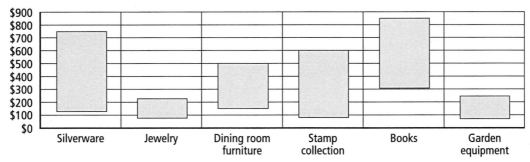

a. Circle the item for which there is the greatest spread. What is this spread?

Answer: The spread on this category is about $_____.

b. Estimate the mean spread for the six categories shown, to the nearest ten.

Answer: The mean spread for the six categories is approximately

$_____.

4. Every three months, *OffTheEstate* closes for a whole month. They tour estate sales and restock their store shelves. What fraction of the year are they closed?

Answer: _____

☆ *Challenge Problem*
You may want to talk this one over with a partner.

A neighbor is giving up his handyman business. He estimates that, over the years, he has paid about $5,000 for all his tools and equipment. He puts his tools and equipment up for sale over a three-day weekend. On the first day of the sale, someone offers him $4,000 to take it all off his hands, as is. What would you do?

_____

_____

_____

♠ A Card Game (for Two or More Players)

The goal of this game is to find the missing number. First, you pick a card. Then you make a calculation to find the answer. The decimal number equals the numerator divided by the denominator.

Materials

What's the Missing Number? Cards (on the next page), and a recording sheet

Directions

1. Shuffle the *What's the Missing Number?* cards, and place them face down in the center of the table. Start a recording sheet with the name of each player at the top of a column. Sit with players around the table.

2. Player 1 picks the top card, reads the two given numbers, and discards the card.

3. All players calculate the missing number (either numerator or denominator). The first player to get the correct answer gets two points. If there is a tie, both players get two points. A player who gets the wrong answer loses a point. If there is a disagreement, work the problem together and decide who has the correct answer. Keep a running total for each player's score.

4. Players take turns picking a card and reading the two given numbers. When all the cards in the deck are gone, shuffle the discard deck and use it again.

5. The winner is the player with the most points. Discuss how you can change the game, make new cards, and try it out!

✏ Before you play the game, try these warm-up problems.

1. Daren picks a card with a decimal number 0.40 and denominator of 35. Colby says the answer is 14. Brandon says the answer is 87.5. Who is correct? Explain.

   Answer: _____

2. Chad picks a card with a decimal number 0.25 and numerator of 9. What is the denominator?

   A 2.25   **B** 5   **C** 18   **D** 36

What's the Missing Number? Cards

Make *What's the Missing Number?* cards for the following pairs of numbers:

Decimal number	Denominator
0.05	100
0.10	50
0.15	20
0.20	8
0.25	12
0.30	9
0.40	35
0.50	60
0.60	20
0.75	4
0.80	45
0.90	30
1.25	16

Decimal number	Numerator
0.05	200
0.10	20
0.15	3
0.20	7
0.25	9
0.30	27
0.40	16
0.50	63
0.60	42
0.75	90
0.80	12
0.90	18
1.25	15

Decimal number	Denominator
0.75	4

Decimal number	Numerator
0.75	3

Decimal number	Numerator
0.30	3

Decimal number	Denominator
0.80	45

Make more cards with your own numbers!

Cars, Clothes, & Books

Example When Jason started his own business, he bought two repossessed cars for a total of $750. He sold one of the cars right away for $850. One year later, he sold the second car for $500, and bought a third car for $600.

a. What is the mean (average) amount of money that Jason paid per car for the three cars?

b. What is the mean amount of money per car that he sold the two cars for?

c. How much has it cost him to own these three cars (ignoring any upkeep costs)?

Solve

Step 1: Add up the total amount of money that Jason paid for the three cars. Then divide by 3.

($750 + $600) = $1,350
$1,350 ÷ 3 = $450

Step 2: Add up the amount of money that Jason sold two of the cars for. Then divide by 2.

($850 + $500) ÷ 2 = $675

Step 3: Subtract the amount of money Jason paid for the cars from the amount that he sold them for.

$1,350 − $1,350 = $0

Answer the Question

Step 4: **a.** Jason paid an average of $450 for each car.
b. He sold the cars for an average of $675 each.
c. It cost Jason nothing to own these three cars!

✏️ Now try these problems.

1. Tova buys two second-hand cars for a total of $1,000. He sells one right away for $900. One year later, he sells the second car for $800, and buys a third car for $600.

a. What is the mean (average) amount of money that Tova pays for the three cars?

Answer: Tova pays an average of $_____ for each car.

b. What is the mean amount of money that he sells the cars for?

Answer: He sells the cars for an average of $_____ each.

c. How much does it cost him to own these three cars?

Answer: Tova makes/loses $_____ on these three cars.

2. Janae takes her niece's baby clothes to the *AChildAgain* shop. The shop buys brand 1 clothes at one fourth of the market value. They buy brand 2 at one third of the market value, brand 3 at one half of the market value. The graph shows brand 1. Plot the graph for brands 2 and 3.

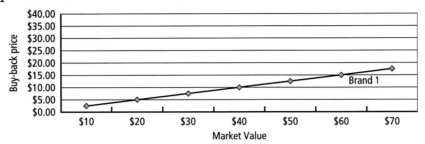

3. Penny records data for the annual book sale. Half way through the sale, she estimates the fraction of books that will sell. How many books does Penny expect to sell? How much money does she expect to make? Complete the chart to show the estimates.

Price per book	25 cents/book	50 cents/book	$1/book
Total number for sale	560	400	380
Estimated fraction of books that will sell	$\frac{3}{4}$	$\frac{3}{5}$	$\frac{1}{2}$
Estimate of number that will sell			
Estimated money made			

☆ Challenge Problem
You may want to talk this one over with a partner.

The book sale has 560 books on sale at 25 cents each, 400 books on sale at 50 cents each, and 380 books on sale at $1 each. You select one book without knowing the price. What price book are you most likely to pick? Why?

Answer: You are most likely to pick a _____ book.

Why? _____

Example Moyna cuts eight circles out of different greeting cards. She folds each circle so that it creates a triangle whose vertices touch the circumference of the circle. She glues four circles together along the side folds to form the top of a three-dimensional hanging decoration. Then she glues four circles together to form the bottom of the decoration. Finally she glues the top to the bottom along the free side folds of the top and bottom. How many triangular faces and side folds does Moyna's hanging decoration have?

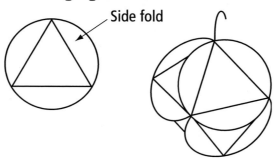

Side fold

Solve

Step 1: Write a sentence that tells how many circles Moyna uses to form one figure.

She glues four circles together to form the top of one figure, and four circles together to form the bottom of the figure.

Step 2: Now deduce the number of triangular faces that a figure has.

The figure uses eight circles.

Each circle has one triangle.

Therefore the figure has eight triangular faces.

Step 3: Calculate the number of side folds that the figure has.

$8 \times 3 = 24$ Eight circles each have three side folds.

$24 \div 2 = 12$ Side folds are glued together.

Answer the Question

Step 4: Moyna's figure has 8 triangular faces, and 12 side folds.

✏️ Now try these problems.

1. Rica cuts eighteen circles out of greeting cards. She folds each circle to make a triangle whose vertices touch the circumference. She glues three circles together along the side folds to form the top of a solid figure. Then she glues three circles together to form the bottom of the figure. Finally she glues the top to the bottom together along the free side folds. Explain in words how to find the number of solid figures that she can make from the remaining circles.

   Answer: _____

2. Bob reuses about $\frac{4}{5}$ of the envelopes that he receives through the mail. He turns them inside out and relabels them. Over the weekend he receives 15 envelopes. About how many can he reuse?

   A 3   **B** 6   **C** 9   **D** 12

3. Elan is a third-generation recycler. He finds videotapes, books, televisions, microwave ovens, low-cost jewelry, clothes, furniture, and even money that has been thrown away. The value of his recycling increases by about 10% from one year to the next. This year he retrieves about $2,450-worth of items. Write and solve an equation to find the approximate value of his recycling two years from now.

   Answer: _____ = $ _____

4. Natane surveys the high school for ways to reuse plastic covers for cans. The top four ideas capture $\frac{5}{6}$ of the student votes. Draw a circle graph to compare this fraction to the fraction of student votes that capture the remaining votes.

☆ *Challenge Problem*
You may want to talk this one over with a partner.

The product of two positive integers is 100. Neither integer is divisible by 10. What is the sum of the two integers? What strategy did you use to find your answer? Is this the only solution to the problem?

Answer: _____

_____

Unit 8

Review

Review What You Learned

In this unit you have used mathematics to solve many problems. You have used mental math and estimation, practiced basic operations, and solved equations. You have also used statistics and probability, ratios and proportions, and graphs.

These two pages give you a chance to review the mathematics you used and check your skills.

✔ Check Your Skills

1. The Rangers hold a yard sale on four different days for three weeks to raise funds for new equipment. They plot the number of items they sell on each day.

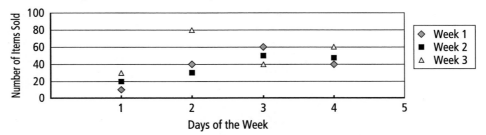

   a. Which day of the week was the peak selling day each week?

   Answer: The peak selling days were _____

   _____

   b. If they drop one day out of the four, which day should they drop and why?

   Answer: They should drop day _____ because _____

   _____

   If you need to review, return to lesson 1 (page 93).

2. At an estate sale, Finn buys a home gym for $150. After three months, he still hasn't used it. He sells it for $200. How much money does he make? What is the percent profit?

   A $50; 25%   **C** $200; 25%

   B $50; 33.3%   **D** $200; 33.3%

   If you need to review, return to lesson 2 (page 95).

3. Hilton buys two second-hand cars for a total of $600. He sells one of the cars right away for $800. One year later, he sells the second car for $400, and buys a third car for $700.

a. What is the mean (average) amount of money that Hilton pays per car for the three cars?

Answer: $_____

b. What is the mean amount of money per car that he sells the cars for?

Answer: $_____

c. How much has it cost him to own these three cars?

Answer: $_____

If you need to review, return to lesson 4 (page 99).

4. Harmoni cuts six circles out of construction paper. She folds each circle so that it creates a triangle whose vertices touch the circumference of the circle. She glues three circles together along the side folds to form the top half of a three-dimensional solid figure. Then she glues three circles together along the side folds to form the bottom half of the figure. Finally she glues the top to the bottom along the free side folds. How many triangular faces and side folds does Harmoni's figure have?

Side fold

Answer: Harmoni's figure has _____ triangular faces and _____ side folds.

If you need to review, return to lesson 5 (page 101).

Write Your Own Problem ✍️

Choose a problem you liked from this unit. Write a similar problem using a situation and related facts from your own life. With a partner, share and solve these problems together. Discuss the mathematics and compare the steps you used. If you need to, rewrite or correct the problems. Write your edited problem and the answer here.

_____

_____

_____

To the Teacher

Welcome to *Smart Shopping,* Book 5 of the *21st Century Lifeskills Mathematics* series.

Mastery of practical math skills is the overarching goal of the *21st Century Lifeskills Mathematics* series. To this end, each of the six books has been carefully designed to present topics students are likely to encounter in everyday life. Each book includes problems that involve estimation, equations, mental math, calculators, and critical thinking. Each book includes additional concept-specific skills such as graphing, averages, statistics, ratios, and measurement.

The books are appropriate for use with small groups, a full class, or by independent learners. The self-explanatory nature of the lessons frees the teacher for individual instruction. Each unit begins with a preview lesson, which models and explains the types of problems students will encounter in the unit. Then there are five lessons, at least one of which is a game. Game titles are italicized in the Table of Contents, on the lesson pages, and in the Answer Key. Each unit ends with a review of the unit concepts. Both illustrations and graphic art are used to support the instruction and maintain interest. A variety of problem types and games are used to sharpen critical thinking skills throughout the program.

Below are the titles of the other books in the *21st Century Lifeskills Mathematics* series:

Book 1: Everyday Life
Book 2: Home & School
Book 3: On the Job
Book 4: Budgeting & Banking
Book 6: Sports, Hobbies, & Recreation

Students from middle school through adult classes will appreciate the practical content of each book.

Through modeling, practice, and review, students will build their math skills and learn to approach everyday mathematical situations with confidence. *21st Century Lifeskills Mathematics* will help your students become successful problem solvers!

Smart Shopping

Answer Key

Unit 1: Retail & Wholesale

Lesson 1: Retail Deals

1. a.

Number of Lenses	Sum of Individual Costs	Total Cost
1	$168.75	$168.75
2	$168.75 + $112.50	$281.25
3	$168.75 + $112.50 + $75	$356.25

b. $50

2.

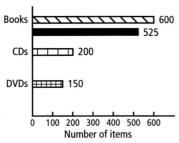

$1,050; 525

3. C $380.00

4. Circle 4 p.m.

Challenge Problem. Each graph is a straight line. The graph for corn that costs $1.00 per ear has a slope of 100 and is twenty times as steep as that of the other graph, which has a slope of 5.

Lesson 2: Visiting the Outlets

1. $\frac{s}{8} = \frac{4}{16}$; $s = \frac{4}{16} \times 8$, so $s = 2$

2. Fraction of DVDs that Marcile will buy =

$$\frac{\text{Number of CDs she buys}}{\text{total number of DVDs}} =$$

$\frac{7}{28}$, or $\frac{1}{4}$

3. Write $6.75 in the blank.

4. D 4

Challenge Problem. $32.89

Lesson 3: Liquidation and Closeouts

1. $104.81 − $3.00 = $101.81; $20.36

2. a. ÷, ×, 20%

b. No. The promise is off by 5%.

3. B $\frac{1}{3}$

4. Circle $225, 66.7%, and $254.

Challenge Problem. $3.875; $0.97

Lesson 4: *Strategic Purchases*

1. 12

2. A 20; No adjacent four open spaces on the board match the shapes of the remaining purchase coupons.

Lesson 5: Co-ops & Clubs

1. a. peanut butter; co-op; 76.8%; supermarket

b. supermarket; $1.55

2. The circle graph shows one sector that is one third of the circle. This sector is labeled as the portion of the population that has membership in a co-operative.

3. D $675

4. $700

Challenge Problem. 2

Review

1.

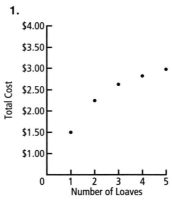

The mean cost per loaf decreases as the number of loaves increases.

2. Fraction of battery-powered hand drills that satisfies his needs is the number of satisfactory hand drills divided by the total number of hand drills: $d = \frac{3}{6}$, or $\frac{1}{2}$

3. D $90

4. a. slacks; 67.8%

b. both stores; $15.26 (co-op club); $1.64 (retail store)

Unit 2: Reading Ads

Lesson 1: Misleading Data

1. Answers may vary. The mean and the median are both $55. But the statement could be interpreted to mean that most people (mode) donated $55. The list shows that most people donated either $100 or $10. Actually, no one donated $55.

2. A The majority of journeys start and end within 25 miles of home.

3. Sample answer: She took the ad literally. She forgot the cost of shipping and handling.

4. D The total student population is ignored.

Challenge Problem. Sample answer: Because it exaggerates the trend in absenteeism, both positive and negative.

Lesson 2: Reading the Classifieds

1. a. 8

b. $157.14

c. half of $9,600 or $4,800

2. B 4,000 miles

3. $\frac{20}{25}$, or $\frac{4}{5}$

4. Circle $47,700

Challenge Problem.

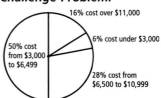

Lesson 3: Everyday Ads

1. a. ($30.50 × 50) − ($27 × 50)

b. makes; $175

2. They must spend at least $15.00, order a large pizza, and have the food delivered on or by 7/1.

3. A $4.75

Unit 2 (continued)

4. Circle the hot dog buns and franks.

Challenge Problem. $20; For a purchase of $20 or more of other products, the tube of toothpaste is free.

Lesson 4: Reading the Fine Print

1. **a.** $111.49
   b. Clem assumed that the second pair he picked would be at half price. He didn't read the fine print to see how the store meant "second pair."
2. C equal to or more than $1,058
3. **a.** $(249.99 \times 0.9) - \$15$
   b. $249.99
4. Circle $203.81

Challenge Problem. 4; -1×-100; -2×-50; -4×-25; -5×-20

Lesson 5: *Stretching Dollars*

1. At the intersection of $40 and 1.
2. C $60

Review

1. The reader could interpret that most people made a donation of $100. This interpretation is wrong. Most people donated $5. The median donation was $40.
2. n; C; 15; $107.14
3. **a.** $(\$29 \times 25) - (\$29.50 \times 25)$
   b. loses; $12.50
4. C $26.45

Unit 3: Rental Sales

Lesson 1: On Vacation

1. **a.** $15
   b. Up to $20 OFF a Weekend or Weekly Rental! $15 OFF! Any Car! Any Day!
2.

Package	Percent of rentals	Total bikes	Total binoculars	Total rentals
Bikes n' Binoculars	60%	84	84	84
Just Bikes	30%	42	0	42
Just Binoculars	10%	0	14	14
Total	100%	126	98	140

3. D $1,140
4. $293.46

Challenge Problem. No. The ratio of rates on the beach is $\frac{5}{2}$. The ratio of rates three blocks off the beach is $\frac{17}{3}$.

Lesson 2: Renting Movies

1. **a.** 20 hours; **b.** $2.50
2. Circle five videocassettes.
3. $\$0.25 \times 2 + \$0.25 \times 1 = \$0.75$
4. D $1.25n + 0.75s = 125$

Challenge Problem. Circle $\frac{25}{16}$ and 25.

Lesson 3: *Rented Out!*

1. $\frac{1}{15}$
2. A A $15 rental is not profitable.

Lesson 4: Temporary Help

1. B The number of days is more than 5.
2. **a.** $2,650
   b. No; does not
   c. $900
3. Circle $2,100
4. Sample equation: $\$56,000 \times 94\% = \$52,640$

Challenge Problem. **a.** $\frac{3}{5}$;
b. $436.67

Lesson 5: Renting Your Home

1. **a.** summer
   b. summer, fall, spring, winter
2. Thayne chooses 3 from A and 1 from C.
3. C $720
4. Show $350.

Challenge Problem. r is the smallest quantity. Explanations may vary. A key point is that the answer to each expression is the same. So you can compare the relationship of the quantities to this answer on a number line.

Review

1. $20 plus club discount
2. B 24 hours; $1.25
3. The weekly rate costs less if Jami hires Isha for more than 15 hours per week at the hourly rate.
4. spring, summer, fall, winter

Unit 4: Buying on Layaway

Lesson 1: All Sorts of Items to Layaway

1. 80% of $99; $79.20; $60 \div 15 = 4$; $\$79.20 \div 4 = \$19.80$
2. Rusty's layaway payments
   a. $49.99; **b.** $299.94
3. 10
4. Circle one friend.

Challenge Problem. Answers will vary. Pros include no interest payments since you do not own the furniture until it is paid for in full. Cons include forfeiting your money if you do not meet the payment plan.

Lesson 2: Terms & Conditions

1. **a.** $56
   b. $11; higher
   c. The layaway time ensures a minimum monthly payment of at least $56.
2. $0.9 \times \$480 \div \$20 = 22$; $\$480 - \$50 \div \$50 = 9$; Kimball cannot meet the conditions of the plan if he pays by check.
3. B 7 months

Challenge Problem. 43; $\frac{x-3}{9} = 15$; so $x = 138$; $\frac{138-9}{3} = 43$

Lesson 3: Return Policies

1. Circle line D.
2. A $30 < d < 365$
3. **a.** Yes; **b.** $494.90
4. Total should add to $135.80.

Challenge Problem. Seven (3, 13, 23, 43, 53, 73, 83)

Lesson 4: *Making Payments*

1. C $110
2. He forfeits his item, drops out of the round, and plays again the next round.

Lesson 5: Timing Is the Key

1. C January
2. **a.** $20; $21.60; $1.60; less
   b. 5; 4; 1; more

Smart Shopping   **107**   Answer Key

Unit 4 (continued)

3. Answers will vary. Key factors include the saving gained from buying on sale, the price of buying on layaway, and paying interest on credit card purchases.
4. Circle row B.

Challenge Problem. 625; Sample answer: Each positive integer is one greater than the odd integer in its position in the 25.

Review

1. C $45
2. $2.67 ($40 − $37.33); $37.33
3. Circle line B.
4. 90; 6; $12.75

Unit 5: Getting the Best Deal

Lesson 1: Picking the Time & the Place

1. $29.70 ÷ 8 = $3.71; $54 ÷ 14 = $3.86; $76.50 ÷ 20 = $3.83; $5.25 − $3.71 = $1.54
2. B $\frac{6}{7}$ of $19.99
3. between April and June; the increase is about $45

Challenge Problem. $6,000. The value decreases by $1,000 less than it decreased the previous year.

Lesson 2: *A Matter of Timing*

1. A $40; $460
2. $150

Lesson 3: Vacation Deals

1. a. the same; b. less than 2.

Depart	Return	Average savings per ticket	Final ticket price	Fraction saved
November 25	November 26	$106		
November 26	November 29	$91		
November 25	December 1	$85		
November 26	November 30	$48	$480	$\frac{1}{11}$

3. $521.05

Challenge Problem. Answers will vary. Consider number of people, cost per person, and amount of luggage.

Lesson 4: Trade Show Opportunities

1. A $5
2. $\frac{1}{84}$; $\frac{2}{84}$, or $\frac{1}{42}$
3. A diagram should show $\frac{1}{3}$ of an hour, or 20 minutes per booth.
4. Answers will vary. Key factors include whether the demo and the play-time are long enough to get a sense of the product.

Challenge Problem. 3. They are 239, 349, and 379.

Lesson 5: Getting an Advantage

1. a. Hong Kong dollar; 0.0352
   b. She should have bought Swiss francs on Monday because the rate went up.
2.

Plot a line from the $\frac{1}{2}$-hour mark on the *x*-axis up to the right at a rate of 6 mph.
   a. by looking at where the lines cross
   b. by measuring the vertical distance on the graph at different points in time
3. The only difference is the length of the subscription. The cost per issue is the same ($2.60). The free weeks are there as a distraction.

Challenge Problem. For example: 1354 + 4531 = 5885; or 1285 + 5821 = 7106 + 6017 = 13123 + 32131 = 45254!

Review

1. $48 ÷ 13 = $3.69; $84 ÷ 25 = $3.36; $117 ÷ 37 = $3.16; $1.09
2. The ratio is greatest at the Snow Suites. The ratio at Snow Suites is about $\frac{5}{32}$. The ratio at Snow Suites is about 3 to

10. The ratio at Winter Castle is about 1 to 4.
3. $165
4. B Euro; 0.1419

Unit 6: On-line Shopping

Lesson 1: Making Comparisons

1. a. $130; b. $95; Sample answer: Divide the length of the price-range portion of the bar by 2 and measure the height of the result.
2. B The books were shipped from two different stores.
3. $\frac{2}{3}$ × 1,200 = 800
4. Circle $93.50.

Challenge Problem. No. There is not the same number of black and white squares left over after the two corners are removed.

Lesson 2: *Shopping without Dropping*

1. Five forward (2 + 3)
2. B He is at zero.

Lesson 3: Searching for Special Items

1. $6
2. C $73.75 per hour
3. $65 − ($12 + $5) = $48

Challenge Problem. Red. Hint: Make a chart of all possibilities. If the friend at the back sees two purple hats, she knows that she is wearing a red hat. If the friend in the middle sees a purple hat, she knows that she is wearing a red hat. So the friend closest to the wall must be wearing a red hat.

Lesson 4: What's New?

1. after; 5
2. Diagram should show the year was 1929.
3. Draw a line between athletics and 1976; between softball and 1992; between basketball and 1988; between tennis and 1999.
4. C $\frac{1}{6}$

Unit 6 (continued)

Challenge Problem. d is the smallest. Sample answer: Draw a number line. Plot each variable, a, b, c, d, on the line so that the answer to each expression is zero. Then compare the positions of each variable.

Lesson 5: Consulting the Experts

1. Making lots of money, by 17%
2. **a.** $342 \div 855 \times 100 = 40\%$; $273 \div 455 \times 100 = 60\%$
   b. do not; 23%; more; 36%; more
3. **a.** 35% (43 − 8%)
   b. Election of a female president, equality for men and women, and a cure for AIDS/cancer. The bars for these events extend to the right of the 40% mark on the x-axis.

Challenge Problem. ($72 \times 1.25) \div 0.9 = \$100$

Review

1. **a.** $140
   b. $\frac{\$55 + \$120}{2} = \$87.50$;
   $\frac{\$75 + \$120}{2} = \$97.50$;
   $10
2. [$4 + 2 \times (\$5 + \$6 + \$9) + \$13] / 8 = \$7
3. Sample answer: Draw a number line. Mark the years 2002 and 1912 on the line. Now mark 80 years back from 2002. Mark and label the segment of the line that shows the difference in years. The difference is 10 years.
4. Circle "Comfortable with one's body." The difference is 15%.

Unit 7: Shopping for a Neighbor

Lesson 1: In Their Shoes

1. A $\frac{1}{4}$
2. $2 \div 8 \times 4 = 1$

3.

Book	Book-sale price	Regular price	Estimated savings
One new release	$4	$21 each	$17.00
Three hardbacks	75 cents each	$15 each	$42.75
5 paperbacks	25 cents each	$5 each	$23.75
10 *History-in-Fiction* magazines	$3 total	$2 each	$17.00
TOTAL SAVINGS			$100.50

4. 225

Challenge Problem. 1 in 7776; The probability of tossing a 6 is $\frac{1}{6}$. So the probability of tossing a 6 five times is $\frac{1}{6} \times \frac{1}{6} \times \frac{1}{6} \times \frac{1}{6} \times \frac{1}{6}$.

Lesson 2: Following Their Lists

1. **a.** $(2, 1, \frac{1}{2}, 1\frac{1}{4}, 2, 1, 1\frac{3}{4}, 1, 2)$
   b. 1 mile
2. C 1 hour 50 minutes
3.

Book	Book-sale price	Regular price	Estimated savings
One new release	$4	$21 each	$17.00
Three hardbacks	75 cents each	$15 each	$42.75
5 paperbacks	25 cents each	$5 each	$23.75
10 *History-in-Fiction* magazines	$3 total	$2 each	$17.00
TOTAL SAVINGS			$100.50

Challenge Problem. 2

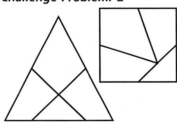

Lesson 3: Price or Quantity

1. **a.** $1; $2; $3; $4
   b. Add $1 for each larger quantity.
   c. $100 \times \$5 = \$500$
   d. The price for 100 items would be the same as the price for 50 items!
2. **a.** $2; **b.** $3
3. Diagram shows 60 cartons ($3 \times 4 \times 5$).

Challenge Problem. 34 and 55; Add the two previous consecutive numbers to get the next number.

Lesson 4: Being a Good Neighbor

1. Number line shows that she gets home at about 7 p.m.
2. 11 a.m.
3. B $8.64

4. 20 minutes $\times$ 3/2 = 30 minutes

Challenge Problem. Answers may vary. Key factors include the price per wash, vacuum, and polish, and whether your neighbor likes discounts like this and will use the coupon.

Lesson 5: *Match It!*

1. next to one of the > 15 open ends
2. A Wait for another *Match It!* card.

Review

1. $\frac{1}{6}$
2. **a.** 11 miles; **b.** 5 miles
3.

	One item	5 items	10 items	50 items	100 items
☐ You save	$2	$15	$40	$250	$600
☐ You pay	$8	$35	$60	$250	$400

4. $3\frac{1}{2}$ hours

Unit 8: Second Time Around

Lesson 1: Garage Sales

1. 2; 1; 4
2.

Week Number	Number of Items Sold
1	180
2	230
3	165

increasing
3. 12.5%
4. A $5

Challenge Problem. 17 + 70 − 65 = 22 years ago

Lesson 2: Estate & Other Sales

1. **a.** $40; **b.** 66.67%
2. D 300%
3. **a.** Circle silverware. $625
   b. $390
4. $\frac{1}{4}$ (or 3 out of every 12 months)

Challenge Problem. Answers will vary. Key factors include how critical it is to get rid of everything, and whether he thinks that he can get more money for it piecemeal by waiting for other buyers.

Unit 8 *(continued)*

Lesson 3: *What's the Missing Number?*

1. Colby is correct. The missing numerator is 0.40×35.
2. C 36

Lesson 4: Cars, Clothes, & Books

1. **a.** $533.33
   b. $850
   c. makes $100

2.

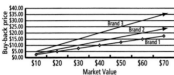

The line graph for brand 2 goes from ($10, $3.33) to ($70, $23.33). The line graph for brand 3 goes from ($10, $5) to ($70, $35).

3.

Price per book	25 cents/ book	50 cents/ book	$1/ book
Total number for sale	560	400	380
Estimated fraction of books that will sell	$\frac{3}{4}$	$\frac{3}{5}$	$\frac{1}{2}$
Estimate of number that will sell	420	240	190
Estimated money made	$105	$120	$190

Challenge Problem. 25-cent book; The probability of picking this book is higher because more books are on sale at that price than at any other price.

Lesson 5: Recycling Trash

1. Sample answer: Subtract the number of circles that she uses for the first figure. Then divide the remainder by the number of faces per figure.
2. D 12
3. Sample answer: $2,450 $\times 1.10^2 = \$2,964.50$
4. The circle graph shows six equal sectors. Five sectors together represent the top four ideas. The remaining one sector shows the other ideas.

Challenge Problem. 29; Sample answer: Test and check. Yes, this is the only solution.

Review

1. **a.** day 3 in weeks 1 and 2; and day 2 in week 3.
   b. Answers may vary. Sample answers: day 3 because sales drop from week to week; or, day 1 because sales are lower than on the other days
2. B $50; 33.3%
3. **a.** $433.33
   b. $600
   c. $100
4. 6; 9